THREE SISTERS

by

Anton Chekhov

a new version by
Susan Coyne

with an introductory essay by
Ronald Bryden

CSPI ✹
CANADIAN SCHOLARS' PRESS INC.

Shaw
The Academy of the Shaw Festival

National Library of Canada Cataloguing in Publication
Chekhov, Anton Pavlovich, 1860-1904
    Three sisters / by Anton Chekhov ; a new version by Susan
Coyne ; with an introductory essay by Ronald Bryden.
Translation of: Tri sestry.
Co-published by: Canadian Scholars' Press Inc.
ISBN 0-9699478-6-0 (Academy of the Shaw Festival).—
ISBN 1-55130-232-2 (Canadian Scholars' Press Inc.)
    I. Coyne, Susan II. Academy of the Shaw Festival III. Title.

PG3456.T8C69 2003   891.72'3   C2003-901902-0

Co-published in 2003 by
The Academy of the Shaw Festival
P.O. Box 774
Niagara-on-the-Lake, Ontario L0S 1J0
www.shawfest.com

and

Canadian Scholars' Press Inc.
180 Bloor Street West, Suite 801
Toronto, Ontario M5S 2V6
www.cspi.org

CSPI gratefully acknowledges financial support from the Government of Canada through the Book Publishing Industry De-
velopment Program (BPIDP) and the Government of Ontario
through the Ontario Book Initiative.

Adapted from a translation by Yana Meerzon and Dmitri Priven
Edited by Denis Johnston
Page layout by Jean German
Cover design by Scott McKowen, cover photo by David Cooper

03   04   05   06   07   08   7   6   5   4   3   2   1

Printed and bound in Canada by AGMV Marquis Imprimeur Inc.

Canadä

A Town Something Like Perm

by Ronald Bryden

In the autumn of 1900, Anton Chekhov wrote his friend Maxim Gorky that he was working on a new play about three young women living in a provincial town "something like Perm". It helps to understand *Three Sisters*, the play he was working on, if you know a thing or two about the town he had in mind.

Chekhov knew that Perm would be familiar to Gorky, who had spent part of his vagabond youth washing dishes on the steamboats that plied the Volga River system. Perm is the largest town on the Kama River, fourth longest in Europe, which collects the run-off from the western slopes of the Ural Mountains and empties it into the Volga below Kazan. "You have a wide, splendid river," says Colonel Vershinin, new commander of the artillery regiment quartered in the town in Chekhov's play. "Yes, but it's cold here," replies Olga Prozorov, eldest daughter of the garrison's late commander, "and there are mosquitoes." Perm lies on the same latitude as Fort McMurray in northern Alberta, ten degrees below the Arctic Circle. It's easy to imagine a similar conversation there about the Athabasca River as it flows north to join the Mackenzie.

Chekhov had spent a long day in Perm on April 27, 1890, waiting for a train to take him over the Urals to Tiumen, railhead of the infant Trans-Siberian Railway. He was on his way to the far end of the Russian Empire, to write about conditions on the prison island of Sakhalin in the Pacific. It had taken him six days travelling on trains and riverboats to cover the twelve hundred miles from Moscow to Perm, and it would take him another seventy-five days to reach Sakhalin. This may help to explain why the Prozorov sisters feel so far from their native city and all that they think of as civilization. In a town like Perm, they could be forgiven for thinking of their place of exile as the last gasp of Europe, the final outpost on the frontier between Europe and Asia, Russia and Siberia.

Long before it had a name or became a town, the river bank where Perm stood had been a jumping off place for Siberia. The Stroganoff family, who held imperial monopolies on salt and furs from Ivan the Terrible, brought loads here from over the Urals to ship down the Kama. It was from here in 1581 that an army of Cossack irregulars, engaged by the Stroganoffs to stop Tatar raids on their caravans, crossed the mountains to destroy the Tatar Khan of Siberia's capital on the river Irtysh, and then, fighting over bog, taiga and tundra for thousands of miles, made their way to the Pacific, an adventure as extraordinary as any achieved by the Spanish conquistadors in the Americas.

Perm, founded in the eighteenth century by a friend of Peter the Great, the mining engineer V.N. Tattischev, became known as the place the empire's salt came from, and its inhabitants, who made their livings hoisting salt-sacks onto barges, as "the salty-eared Permyaks". It was Tattischev who took pity on them and had the idea of bringing together the Urals' wealth of wood and iron in a cooperage, making barrels and casks for the river trade. On that foundation grew shipyards, machine shops and even an arms factory – a giant cannon made to celebrate Alexander III's coronation in 1873 still sits in a park above the Kama and has an entry in the Guinness Book of Records. A professor coming from St Petersburg to help launch a university in 1916, twelve years after Chekhov's death, described what he found as "a provincial town peacefully sleeping in the anteroom of culture."

Because of its frontier history as the gate to Siberia, Perm was from early on a garrison town. It tells something that Chekhov chose it as his background for *Three Sisters*, his main study of the place of the military in Russian life. It was on his journey to Sakhalin that he discovered the extent to which the army was the instrument that held the empire together. He never said publicly whether he thought the empire a good thing – he had no wish to return to Siberia – though he envied the modernization that imperialism had brought to Hong Kong and Singapore, stops on his way home from Sakhalin. But you didn't have to approve of the empire to admire the ill-rewarded service of the men who mapped the Asian wilderness, defended Russia's border with China on the Amur, and kept order in the far-flung outposts of the largest country on earth, with little hope of ever seeing their homes again.

"It maybe different elsewhere," says Masha, the middle Prozorov sister, to Colonel Vershinin, "but in our town all the finest people, the best-educated and the most decent, are in the military." She is flattering the man with whom she is falling in love, as well as herself – she still thinks of herself as a general's daughter rather than a teacher's wife – but although none of his garrison officers is brilliant intellectually, Chekhov seems to agree with her. He had been surprised by the intellectual level of the army posts he passed through along the Amur, and knew that army officers were better educated than most Russian citizens. Peter the Great had made that part of his plan when he created the Russian army in the eighteenth century. Common soldiers must learn to read weapon manuals, officers must attend special cadet schools. Like aristocrats and courtiers, members of the army were personal servants of the emperor. To signal this, Peter required them like his courtiers to go clean-shaven in the Western manner, shedding the full beards that traditional Russian males regarded as their pious duty to display. (Tolstoy in *War and Peace* writes of peasant boys being "taken and shaven for a soldier".) There's a piteous piece of comedy near the end of *Three Sisters* when the schoolmaster Kulygin comes on clean-shaven. He is volunteering to replace his wife's lover after the garrison's departure. Masha cries, laughs when he dons a false beard he confiscated from a pupil, then cries again.

Peter the Great designed an army which would have no loyalties to anything but the empire and its emperors. To create it, he conscripted Russian peasant boys from their villages – none of the mercenaries and criminals which made up most European armies – and made them soldiers for life, never to see their homes again. The army itself became their home, their family. Each unit formed an *artel*, modelled on village collectives, to be a kind of bank and commissariat, to make up any deficiencies in food, clothing or transport. Perpetually underfunded, regiments were expected to be self-sufficient, producing their own bakers, blacksmiths, carpenters, saddlers, tailors and wheelwrights, and to sell their skills to enrich the *artel* when necessary. A regiment in Saratov, down the Volga, ran a profitable sideline in undertaking, making coffins and hiring out horses and mourners for funerals. Lieutenant Rohde in

Three Sisters teaches gymnastics at the local high school. His salary may enable him to buy flowers for Irina's name day, but most of it probably goes into the garrison's general fund.

To ensure that garrisons didn't go native, bonding with the local population, they were always quartered outside towns, in their own fortress or kremlin. Between the town and the kremlin would grow up a suburb or quarter housing other people with official connections to the state – in effect, a colony of the taxers maintaining a certain distance from the taxed. The Prozorov girls in *Three Sisters* obviously live in such a suburb, while Vershinin and the other officers clearly maintain quarters nearby outside the kremlin; but whereas in towns further west the houses would be built of brick and stone, reflecting the wealth of the untaxed, in this town they seem to be built of wood, like the towns in Siberia – fire destroys a whole street overnight, and would probably have spread further but for the action of the garrison, carrying water from the river up through the Prozorovs' garden.

In many ways, the garrison is an occupying power, there to enforce the will of the emperor on the populace if necessary. (Perm was to be one of the hotbeds of the 1905 revolution.) Chekhov shows little sympathy for Natasha, the local girl who marries Andrei Prozorov and gradually drives his sisters from their house, and he makes it clear she is a thoroughly unlikeable human being. But from her own point of view, she is something like an Irish girl in the nineteenth century, married into a family of "ascendancy" British who keep trying to correct her manners and accent. The revenge she takes on the Prozorovs is terrible, but she has cause for revenge.

Above all, the empire made sure its garrisons didn't go native by moving them regularly. At the end of *Three Sisters*, the artillery brigade which has been quartered on the town for more than fifteen years is transferred to Poland – there is no longer any threat of war on the old Siberian frontier, but clouds are gathering in the Far East and in the west, on the Polish frontier with Germany. The garrison marches away, except for Solyony's battery, which goes down-river by barge, and the sisters are left behind, unable to understand what life has done to them.

You could compare them to bees left behind when their hive has been moved. I had a friend who put himself through college working for a bee farmer who rented his hives to the fruit farmers of the Niagara peninsula. For several weeks in the spring he would drive a truck of hives from orchard to orchard, setting the hives under the trees as they came into blossom to do the work of pollination for which the local bee population was insufficient. At the end of the week, he claimed, you could hear the bees singing with satisfaction in their hives, but there were always a few bees left outside, flying in bewildered circles, their places in the world gone forever. They could never live apart from their hives. One cold spring night would be enough to carry them off. It made you shudder, my friend said.

Chekhov admired much about the imperial army, but he could not overlook that it was part of the state and its apparatus, not of Russia. It contributed its share to the process he had observed in his own home town of Taganrog, on the Sea of Azov – the centralization of the empire was gradually stripping the provinces of their best young men (including the five Chekhov brothers), leaving whole districts overpopulated with young women unable to find suitable husbands, sending regiments of young males to the far ends of the earth. The best world for humans, as for bees, is one in which everyone is at home, but the century of great empires in which he lived had created one in which more and more people were displaced and homesick. That was another of the lessons he had brought back from Sakhalin.

Ronald Bryden was Literary Adviser to the Shaw Festival from 1992 to 2002. He has also been dramaturge to Britain's Royal Shakespeare Company, drama critic of The Observer, *and head of the University of Toronto's Graduate Centre for Study of Drama. His collection* Shaw and His Contemporaries: Theatre Essays *appeared in 2002.*

THREE SISTERS

A drama in four acts

THREE SISTERS

Dramatis Personae

ANDREI PROZOROV
NATASHA, his fiancée, then wife
OLGA
MASHA } his sisters
IRINA
KULYGIN, a schoolteacher, Masha's husband
VERSHININ, battery commander
TUZENBACH, Baron, first lieutenant
SOLYONY, subaltern
CHEBUTYKIN, military doctor
FEDOTIK, second lieutenant
ROHDE, second lieutenant
FERAPONT, District Council caretaker
ANFISA, a nanny, an old woman of 80

The action takes place in a provincial town.

This version of *Three Sisters* was first performed at the Festival Theatre, Niagara-on-the-Lake, on April 26, 2003, with the following cast:

Olga	KELLI FOX
Masha	TARA ROSLING
Irina	CAROLINE CAVE
Chebutykin	DAVID SCHURMANN
Tuzenbach	JEFF MEADOWS
Solyony	PETER KRANTZ
Anfisa	JENNIFER PHIPPS
Ferapont	RICHARD FARRELL
Vershinin	KEVIN BUNDY
Andrei	BEN CARLSON
Kulygin	DOUGLAS E. HUGHES
Natasha	FIONA BYRNE
Fedotik	JEFF MADDEN
Rohde	ANDREW BUNKER
Maid / Musician's Girl	KATHERINE SLATER
Houseboy / Soldier	JARED BROWN
Orderly / Soldier	SAM STRASFELD
Musician / Soldier	GEORGE DAWSON
Soldier	MARK ADRIAANS

Directed by JACKIE MAXWELL

Designed by SUE LePAGE

Lighting designed by KEVIN LAMOTTE

Original music composed by PAUL SPORTELLI

ACT I

A living-room in the Prozorov house in a provincial town. Behind a series of columns, a big dining-room can be seen, where a table is being set for lunch. It is noon; outside it is sunny and bright. OLGA, wearing the blue uniform of a schoolteacher, is walking up and down marking assignments. MASHA, in a black dress, her hat on her lap, is sitting and reading a book. IRINA, in a white dress, is standing. She is deep in thought.

OLGA. It's a year ago that father died, exactly a year, May the fifth, your name day, Irina. It was cold that day, it was snowing. I thought I'd never live through it, and you were lying in a dead faint. But now here it is a year later and we can think about it quite easily, you're dressed in white, your face is radiant...

The clock strikes twelve.

The clock struck twelve then, too. [*Pause.*] I remember them shouldering the coffin, and the band playing, and the rifle salute beside the grave. Father was a general, he had a brigade, but only a few people came. Mind you, it was snowing. Raining hard and snowing.

IRINA. Why keep on about it!

> *Behind the columns, in the dining-room, Baron* TUZENBACH, CHEBUTYKIN, *and* SOLYONY *appear.*

OLGA. It's warm today, we can have the windows open wide, but the leaves on the birch trees aren't out yet. Father got his brigade and we left Moscow eleven years ago, and I remember it all so clearly. In Moscow at this time of year, everything's in bloom, the weather is glorious. Eleven years ago, but I remember it all as if it were yesterday. My God! I woke up this morning, saw the sunlight pouring in, felt the warm spring air, and such a feeling of joy welled up in me, such a longing for Moscow, for home.

CHEBUTYKIN. Like hell you will!

TUZENBACH. Ridiculous, I know.

> MASHA, *deep in thought over her book, whistles a tune to herself.*

OLGA. Don't whistle, Masha. How can you! [*Pause.*] I'm at school all day, and I tutor in the evenings, so my head's always aching and I'm starting to think like an old woman. Four years of teaching and every day I feel my youth and strength draining out of me, drop by drop. And the only thing that grows, the only thing that gets stronger is this one thought, this one desire...

IRINA. Off to Moscow. Sell the house, leave it all, and off to Moscow...

OLGA. Yes! Off to Moscow as soon as we can.

CHEBUTYKIN *and* TUZENBACH *laugh.*

IRINA. Our brother will be a professor, most likely. In any case he won't stay here. The only hitch is poor Masha.

OLGA. Masha will come to Moscow for the whole summer, every year.

MASHA *whistles a song quietly.*

IRINA. God willing, it will all work out. [*Looking through the window.*] What a glorious day! I don't know why I feel so well! This morning when I woke up I remembered it was my name day, and suddenly I felt so excited, and I thought of my childhood, when mama was still alive. Such wonderful thoughts I had, such thoughts!

OLGA. You look beautiful today. Your face is radiant. Masha's looking very pretty, too. Andrei could be good-looking, but he's put on too much weight, it doesn't suit him. As for me, I'm too thin, I look old, because I get so irritated with the girls at school. But today I'm free, I'm home, my headache is gone, I feel younger than I did when I went to bed. I'm only twenty-eight years old.... Everything's for the best, everything is in God's hands, but I think if I were married and stayed home all day, it would be better. [*Pause.*] I would love my husband.

TUZENBACH [*to* SOLYONY]. You're being idiotic, I'm tired of listening to you. [*Entering the living-room.*] I forgot to tell you. Our new battery commander, Colonel Vershinin, is planning to call today. [*Sits down at the piano.*]

OLGA. Well, I'm very pleased.

IRINA. Is he old?

TUZENBACH. No, not really. Forty, forty-five at the most. [*Plays the piano softly.*] Seems a nice fellow. Not stupid – that's for sure. But he talks a lot.

IRINA. Is he interesting?

TUZENBACH. I suppose. But he has a wife, a mother-in-law, and two daughters. It's his second wife, in fact. He comes to call and tells everyone that he has a wife and two daughters. He'll tell you too, I'm sure. His wife is a bit of a nutter, wears a long braid like a schoolgirl, likes to make grand pronouncements, frequently attempts suicide, to spite her husband I think. I would have left her a long time ago, but he puts up with her and just complains.

SOLYONY [*entering from the dining-room with* CHEBUTYKIN]. With one arm I can lift only fifty pounds, but with two arms at least a hundred and seventy. Hence I conclude that two men are not twice as strong as one, but three times or more...

CHEBUTYKIN [*reading a newspaper as he walks*]. Here's a cure for baldness ... two ounces of mothballs in half a bottle of alcohol ... dissolve and use daily... [*Writes in his notebook.*] I'll make a note of that! [*To* SOLYONY.] So, as I was saying, you stick a cork in a bottle, with a little glass tube running through it.... Then you take a pinch of plain, ordinary alum...

IRINA. Ivan Romanych, my dear Ivan Romanych!

CHEBUTYKIN. What is it, my child, my joy?

IRINA. Tell me, why am I so happy today? It's like I'm sailing along, under a big blue sky and huge white birds are soaring overhead. Why is that? Why?

CHEBUTYKIN [*kissing both her hands, gently*]. My own little white bird...

IRINA. I got up this morning, and washed my face, and suddenly everything became clear to me. I thought, "I know how to live." My dear Ivan Romanych, I know the secret. A man must work, he must work in the sweat of his brow whoever he might be, and this alone is the meaning and purpose of his life, his happiness, his bliss. It must be so good to be a road worker, who gets up at the break of day and paves the street, or a shepherd, or a teacher, or an engine driver on a train.... My God, better to be an ox, or a horse, a beast of burden, anything but a young woman, who gets up at noon, has coffee in bed, then takes two hours to get dressed ... that's disgraceful! You know how in hot weather, you long for a cold drink? That's how I feel about work. From now on, if I don't get up early and work, don't be friends with me any more, Ivan Romanych.

CHEBUTYKIN [*tenderly*]. I won't, I won't...

OLGA. Father trained us to get up at seven o'clock. Now Irina wakes at seven, and lies there till at least nine, just thinking. With such a serious look on her face! [*Laughs.*]

IRINA. You still think of me as a little girl, so it's funny to you when I'm being serious. I'm twenty!

TUZENBACH. Longing to work, my God, I know exactly what you mean! I've never worked a day in my whole life. I was born in St Petersburg, that cold and idle city, in a family that never knew work or any kind of hardship. I remember when I would come home from the military college, my servant would pull my boots off while I made a stupid scene, and my mother looked on with adoration and couldn't understand why others failed to do the same. I was sheltered from work. Well, that was a waste of effort! The time is almost here, something great is upon us, a powerful and healthy storm is about to break and when it does it's going to cleanse our society of idleness, indifference, prejudice against work, this rotten boredom. I'm going to work, and in twenty-five or thirty years, everyone will be working. Every single one!

CHEBUTYKIN. Not I.

TUZENBACH. You don't count.

SOLYONY. In twenty-five years you won't be around, thank God. In a couple of years, you'll drop dead from a stroke, or else I'll blow up and put a bullet through your head, my angel. [*Takes out a bottle of perfume and sprinkles some on his chest and hands.*]

CHEBUTYKIN [*laughs*]. And I really have never done anything, ever. Once I graduated from university, I never lifted a finger, I haven't even read a book since then, just newspapers... [*Takes another newspaper out of his pocket.*] For instance ... I know from the newspapers, there was, let's say, a Dobrolubov, but what the heck he wrote – don't know ... haven't the foggiest...

There is a knocking from the floor below.

Ah-hah.... They're calling me downstairs,

there's someone there to see me. I'll be back in a minute ... just wait... [*Leaves in a hurry, brushing his beard.*]

IRINA. He's up to something.

TUZENBACH. Yes. He had such a meaningful look on his face, he's obviously going to bring you a present.

IRINA. It's so embarrassing!

OLGA. Yes, it's appalling. He always manages to make a fool of himself.

MASHA. "Beside the sea a green oak's standing/ and on it hangs a golden chain" ... "and on it hangs a golden chain"... [*stands up and hums quietly.*]

OLGA. You're not much fun today, Masha.

Humming, MASHA *puts on her hat.*

Where are you going?

MASHA. Home.

IRINA. That's odd...

TUZENBACH. Leaving a name day party!

MASHA. Who cares ... I'll be back this evening. Goodbye, my darling... [*Kisses* IRINA.] I wish you health and happiness.... In the old days, when father was alive, we'd have thirty or forty officers at our parties, and everybody would be laughing and carrying on, but to-day there's a person and a half and it's as quiet as the grave.... I'll go ... I'm a bit blue today, a bit down in the dumps, so don't pay any attention. [*Laughing through tears.*] We'll talk later, good-bye till then, my darling, I'll take myself off somewhere.

IRINA [*annoyed*]. Why do you always have to...

OLGA [*tearfully*]. I understand you, Masha.

SOLYONY. If a man philosophizes, it'll be philosophistry or even sophistry, but if a woman or even two women philosophize: woof!

MASHA. And what is that supposed to mean, you bad scary man?

SOLYONY. Nothing. "Before the man had time to breathe, the bear had caught him in a squeeze."

Pause.

MASHA [*to* OLGA, *angrily*]. Don't be such a cry-baby!

Enter ANFISA *and* FERAPONT *with a cake.*

ANFISA. This way, old man. Come on in, your feet are clean. [*To* IRINA.] It's from the District Council, from Mikhail Protopopov.... A cake.

IRINA. Thank you. Thank him for me. [*Takes the cake.*]

FERAPONT. What's that?

IRINA [*louder*]. Thank him from me!

OLGA. Nana, give him some pie. Go on, Ferapont, they'll give you some pie in the kitchen.

FERAPONT. What's that?

ANFISA. Come on, old man. Come with me... [*Exit with* FERAPONT.]

MASHA. I don't care for this Protopopov man. He shouldn't be invited.

IRINA. I didn't invite him.

MASHA. Good.

> *Enter* CHEBUTYKIN, *followed by* SOLDIER *with a silver samovar; a hum of surprise and dismay.*

OLGA [*buries her face in her hands*]. A silver samovar! Oh! That is the limit! [*Exit into the dining-room and goes to the table.*]

IRINA. Ivan Romanych, darling, what are you doing!

TUZENBACH [*laughs*]. Told you!

MASHA. Ivan Romanych, you have absolutely no shame!

CHEBUTYKIN. My dears, my little girls, you are everything to me, the most precious things in this world. I'll be sixty soon, I'm an old man, a lonely, worthless old man.... There's

14

nothing good in me except for this love I have for you, and without you, I'd have died a long time ago... [*To* IRINA.] My darling, my sweet little girl, I've known you since the day you were born.... I carried you in my arms.... I loved your sainted mother...

IRINA. But why must you give such extravagant presents!

CHEBUTYKIN [*through his tears, angrily*]. Extravagant presents.... Get out! [*To his orderly.*] Put the samovar over there... [*Mocking.*] Extravagant presents...

> *The orderly takes the samovar away to the dining-room.*

ANFISA [*passing through the living-room*]. It's a colonel here to see you, children, a stranger! He's just taking off his coat, dears, and then he's coming here. Irinushka, you be nice to the man... [*Exiting.*] Oh, for goodness' sake, it's past time for lunch ... goodness sake...

TUZENBACH. It must be Vershinin.

> *Enter* VERSHININ.

Lieutenant-Colonel Vershinin!

VERSHININ [*to* MASHA *and* IRINA]. Allow me to introduce myself: Vershinin. Such a pleasure to be with you all at last. My, how you've changed! My, my!

IRINA. Please, sit down. We're so happy to meet you.

VERSHININ [*cheerfully*]. Oh indeed. Indeed. Extremely happy! But there are three of you, aren't there? I seem to remember – three girls. I can't picture the faces, but I'm sure I remember that Colonel Prozorov had three little girls – I met you all at his house. Where do the years go?

TUZENBACH. Colonel Vershinin has just arrived from Moscow.

IRINA. From Moscow, you're from Moscow?

VERSHININ. Yes, just arrived. Your father was a battery commander there, and I was an officer in the same brigade. [*To* MASHA.] Your face I seem to remember.

MASHA. I don't remember yours!

IRINA. Olya! Olya! [*Shouts into the dining-room.*] Olya, come quick!

Olga enters the living-room from the dining-room.

Lieutenant-Colonel Vershinin has just arrived from Moscow, it seems.

VERSHININ. So you must be Olga, the eldest ... And you are Masha.... And you must be Irina – the youngest...

Act I

OLGA. Are you really from Moscow?

VERSHININ. Yes. I studied in Moscow and then I entered the service in Moscow, I was there for a long time in fact; finally became a battery commander, and here I am, as you see. I'm afraid I don't remember you clearly, I just remember that you were three sisters. Your father I remember very well, I can close my eyes and see him as if he were still alive. I used to visit you in Moscow...

OLGA. I thought I remembered everybody, but then you say...

VERSHININ. My name is Aleksandr.

IRINA. Aleksandr, and you're from Moscow.... What a surprise!

OLGA. We're moving there, you know.

IRINA. We hope to be there by fall. That's our home town, where we were born.... On Old Basmannaya Street...

The two laugh joyously.

MASHA. Someone from Moscow. Someone from home. [*Lively.*] Now I've got it! Remember, Olya, how we used to talk about the "lovesick major". You were a lieutenant then and you were in love with someone, and for some reason everyone teased you and called you the "lovesick major"...

VERSHININ [*laughs*]. That's it.... The lovesick major, that's me.

MASHA. You only had a moustache back then.... Oh, but you've aged! [*Through her tears.*] How you've aged.

VERSHININ. Yes, when they called me "the lovesick major," I was young and in love. Not any more.

OLGA. But you don't have a single grey hair yet. You've aged, but you're not old.

VERSHININ. Nearly forty-three. Have you been away from Moscow long?

IRINA. Eleven years. Come on, Masha, why are you crying, you silly? [*Through her tears.*] You'll have me crying in a moment...

MASHA. I'm fine. So, what street did you live on?

VERSHININ. On Old Basmannaya.

OLGA. That's where we used to live...

VERSHININ. I lived on Nemetskaya for a while. From Nemetskaya, I used to walk to the Krasny Barracks. There's a kind of dismal-looking bridge on the way, water rushing underneath it. A lonely man can feel quite bereft standing there.

    Pause.

But here, what a wide, splendid river! A splendid river!

OLGA. Yes, but it's cold here. It's cold and there are mosquitoes...

VERSHININ. Don't say it! Such a fine, healthy Russian climate you have here. The forest, the river ... and birch trees! Dear, humble birches, I love them more than any other tree. It must be so good to live here. The only odd thing is that the railway station is twenty miles away.... And nobody knows why.

SOLYONY. I know why.

Everyone looks at him.

Because if it were near, then it wouldn't be far, and if it were far, then it wouldn't be near.

Uneasy silence.

TUZENBACH. What a wag.

OLGA. Now, I've placed you. I remember you now.

VERSHININ. I knew your mother.

CHEBUTYKIN. She was a good woman, God rest her soul.

IRINA. Mama is buried in Moscow.

OLGA. In the Novo-Devichy cemetery...

MASHA. You know, I'm starting to forget her face.

That's how it will be with us, too. We'll be forgotten.

VERSHININ. Yes. We'll be forgotten. That's our fate, nothing you can do about it. In fact, everything that we cling to, all our values, our most cherished ideals – the time will come – when it will all be forgotten or seem hopelessly outdated.

Pause.

The interesting thing is that right now we have no way of knowing what will one day be considered to be serious and significant, and what will seem trite and ridiculous. Didn't Copernicus's or, let's say, Columbus's discovery at first seem a waste of time, and didn't some old drivel written by a fool seem like the truth? And who knows, maybe this life, which we take for granted, in time will seem odd, awkward, puzzling, distasteful, perhaps even wicked.

TUZENBACH. Who knows? Maybe they will think highly of us and remember us with respect. After all, there's no torture now, no executions, no invasions, but of course there still is a great deal of suffering!

SOLYONY [*in a high-pitched voice*]. Cheep-cheep-cheep.... Listen everyone. The Baron's philosophizing. He's on a roll...

TUZENBACH. Vasily, would you please leave me alone... [*Changes his seat.*] Really, it's becoming extremely tiresome.

SOLYONY [*in a high-pitched voice*]. Cheep-cheep-cheep...

TUZENBACH [*to* VERSHININ]. The kind of suffering we see today – and undoubtedly there's a great deal of it – itself demonstrates a certain moral stature that our society has already achieved...

VERSHININ. Yes, yes, of course.

CHEBUTYKIN. You've just said, Baron, that people will think highly of us; yet people are still short. [*Stands up.*] Look how short I am. Go ahead, cheer me up, and tell me you think highly of me.

Violin plays backstage.

MASHA. That's Andrei playing, our brother.

IRINA. He's our scholar. He'll be a professor some day. Papa was a soldier, but his son chose an academic career.

MASHA. It's what Papa wanted for him.

OLGA. We've been teasing him all day. He seems to be a little bit in love.

IRINA. With a certain young lady from around here. She'll probably come by later.

MASHA. You should see what she wears! It's not so much that it's ugly or unfashionable, it's just sort of – woeful. Like, a garish yellow skirt with a fringe, and then a bright red blouse on top. And her cheeks have been scrubbed till they're shiny! Andrei is not in love – I don't believe that, he does have some taste; it's nothing, he's just teasing us, fooling around. I heard yesterday that she's marrying Protopopov, the chair of the local council. That's perfect... [*into the side door*]. Andrei, come in here! Just for a minute, dear!

Enter ANDREI.

OLGA. This is our brother, Andrei.

VERSHININ. Vershinin.

ANDREI. Prozorov. [*Wipes the sweat off his face.*] You're the new battery commander?

OLGA. Can you believe it, the colonel is from Moscow.

ANDREI. Really? Congratulations, now my sisters won't give you a moment's peace.

VERSHININ. I've already managed to bore them.

IRINA. Isn't this a pretty picture frame my brother gave me? [*Shows the frame.*] He made it himself.

VERSHININ [*looking at the frame not knowing what*

to say]. Yes ... it's really ... goodness...

IRINA. And that frame over there, on the piano, he made that too.

> ANDREI *makes a waving gesture with his hand and steps aside.*

OLGA. He's our scholar, and he plays the violin, and he makes things with his hands – he's a man of many talents. Andrei, don't go! He's got this habit – he's always running away. Come here!

> MASHA *and* IRINA *take him by the arms and bring him back, laughing.*

MASHA. Come on!

ANDREI. Please don't.

MASHA. He's so silly! We called Alexandr the "lovesick major," and he didn't mind.

VERSHININ. Not at all!

MASHA. And I'm going to call you "the lovesick fiddler"!

IRINA. Or "the lovesick professor"!

OLGA. He's in love! Andryusha is in love!

IRINA [*clapping her hands*]. Bravo, bravo! Andryushka's in love!

CHEBUTYKIN [*approaches* ANDREI *from behind and puts his hands on* ANDREI*'s waist*]. "Sweet is the Budding Spring of love!" [*He laughs loudly; still holding his newspaper.*]

ANDREI. All right, that's enough everybody. [*Wipes his face.*] I didn't sleep all night, so I'm a bit on edge. I read until four, and then went to bed, but it was no use. I kept tossing and turning, and then with the early sunrise, the sun just poured into my room. I'm going to be home all summer, so I'm planning to translate a book from English.

VERSHININ. You read English?

ANDREI. Yes. Father, God rest his soul, oppressed us with education. It's funny, but I have to admit that after his death I started to put on weight and a year later I'm actually quite heavy, as if I've been let out of confinement. Thanks to Father, my sisters and I know French, German and English, and Irina knows Italian. But at what cost!

MASHA. In this town, knowing three languages is a meaningless luxury. Not even a luxury, it's like some kind of a useless appendage, like a sixth finger. We know far too much.

VERSHININ. What a thing to say! [*Laughs.*] Know too much! I can't imagine the town so primitive and dull, that it wouldn't need intelligent, educated people. Let's imagine, among the hundred thousand inhabitants of this particular backwater, there are only three people like you. Obviously, you can't hope to prevail against the forces of darkness; little by little you'll have to succumb, you'll be overwhelmed, you'll disappear, yes, but not without a trace; in your place, there might come six and then twelve people like you, and on and on, until eventually people like you will make up the majority. In two or three hundred years, life on Earth will be unimaginably wonderful and amazing. This is ultimately what our souls demand, and if this kind of life doesn't yet exist, we must dream of it, hope for it, imagine it; we must see more and understand more than our fathers and grandfathers. [*Laughs.*] And yet you complain that you know too much.

MASHA [*takes off her hat*]. I'm staying for lunch.

IRINA [*with a sigh*]. Really, someone should write all that down...

ANDREI *is gone; he has slipped out.*

TUZENBACH. In the future, you say, life on Earth will be wonderful and amazing. But in order to share in it now, even from a distance, one must prepare for it, one must work...

VERSHININ [*stands up*]. Yes. But what a lot of flowers you have here! [*Looking around.*] And such a lovely room, so full of light and air. I envy you! I mean, I've spent my life hopping between tiny apartments with two chairs, a sofa, and a stove that keeps smoking all the time. What's been missing from my life are these flowers... [*rubs his hands together*]. Oh, well! Never mind!

TUZENBACH. Yes, work. Work is the key. I know you're thinking: "The German is getting sentimental." But I assure you, I'm one hundred percent Russian. I don't even speak German. My father is Orthodox...

Pause.

VERSHININ [*walks about the stage*]. I often think: what if we could start all over again, but this time, fully aware? What if one life, the one we've already lived through, was our rough draft, so to speak, and the other one was the good copy! In that case, I think that each of us would try at all costs not to repeat himself. Certainly, he would arrange his life differently, he would get a house like this one, with flowers, plenty of light.... I have a wife and two girls, and on top of that my wife's not well and so on and anyway, if I had a chance to start over again, I wouldn't get married. No. No, sir!

Enter KULYGIN *in uniform.*

KULYGIN [*approaches* IRINA]. My dear sister-in-law, allow me to congratulate you on your saint's day and wish you sincerely, from the bottom of my heart, good health and everything else a girl your age could wish for. And, may I present you with this little book. [*Gives her the book.*] The history of our high school for the past fifty years, written by me. A poor thing but mine own, written in my spare time, but read it anyway. Good morning, everyone! [*To* VERSHININ.] Kulygin, teacher in the local high school, civil servant of the seventh rank. [*To* IRINA.] In that book, you'll find a list of everyone who has graduated from our school in the past fifty years. *Feci, quand potui, faciat meliora potentes.* "Let those who can do better." [*Kisses* MASHA.]

IRINA. But you already gave me this book, for Easter.

KULYGIN [*laughs*]. No, really?! In that case, give it back to me, or better yet give it to the Colonel. Take it, Colonel. Read it some day, when you've nothing better to do.

VERSHININ. Thank you. [*About to leave.*] I'm so glad to have met you...

OLGA. You're not leaving? No!

IRINA. You're staying for lunch. Please.

OLGA. Please stay!

VERSHININ [*bows*]. I seem to be intruding on a party. I'm sorry, I didn't know, I haven't congratulated you... [*Leaves for the dining-room with* OLGA].

KULYGIN. Ladies and gentlemen, today is Sunday, a day of rest, so let us rest, let us rejoice, everyone according to his age and station. Those rugs will need to be put away for the summer.... With some Persian powder or mothballs.... The Romans were healthy because they knew how to work, and they knew how to take their ease: *mens sana in corpore sano.* Life in Roman times flowed according to established routines. Our principal always says: the main thing in life is its form.... When a thing loses its form, it's finished – it's the same in our everyday life. [*Puts his hands around* MASHA*'s waist, laughing.*] Masha loves me. My wife loves me. The curtains should be put away too.... I'm happy today, I'm in good spirits. Masha, at four this afternoon we're going to the headmaster's. It's an outing for the teachers and their families.

MASHA. I'm not going.

KULYGIN [*saddened*]. But, why?

MASHA. We'll talk later. [*Angrily.*] Fine, I'll go, just leave me alone. [*Goes aside.*]

KULYGIN. And afterwards we're invited to spend the whole evening with the headmaster. In spite of his poor health, that man struggles to be sociable. A brilliant mind. An exceptional human being. Yesterday, after the meeting, he says to me, "You know, Kulygin,

I am so tired! So tired!" [*Looks at the wall clock, then at his watch.*] Your clock is seven minutes fast. "Yes," he says. "I really am tired!"

Someone plays a violin backstage.

OLGA. Ladies and gentlemen, if you please, lunch is served! We've got a pie!

KULYGIN. Ah, my dear, dear Olga! Yesterday I worked from early morning till eleven at night, went to bed exhausted and today I feel happy. [*Goes to the dining-room towards the table*]. My dear...

CHEBUTYKIN [*puts the newspaper in his pocket, combs his beard*]. Pie? Hooray!

MASHA [*to* CHEBUTYKIN, *sternly*]. But listen, you, no drinking today. Do you hear me? Drinking is not good for you.

CHEBUTYKIN. Ha! I'm all better now. Haven't had a binge in two years. [*Impatiently.*] Dear heart, it's all the same.

MASHA. Still, don't you dare drink. Don't you dare. [*Angrily, but making sure* KULYGIN *cannot hear.*] Good Christ, another interminable evening at the headmaster's!

TUZENBACH. I wouldn't go if I were you.... Very simple.

CHEBUTYKIN. Don't go, my sweetheart.

MASHA. Sure, don't go.... This hellish, unbearable life... [*Goes to the dining-room.*]

CHEBUTYKIN [*follows her*]. Well, well!

SOLYONY [*coming through to the dining-room*]. Cheep-cheep-cheep...

TUZENBACH. That's enough, Solyony. Stop it!

SOLYONY. Cheep-cheep-cheep...

KULYGIN [*cheerfully*]. To your health, Colonel! I'm a teacher and part of the family, Masha's husband. She's a nice nice girl, very nice...

VERSHININ. I'll have some of this dark vodka... [*Drinks.*] Cheers! [*To* OLGA.] I feel so at ease with all of you!...

There are only IRINA *and* TUZENBACH *in the living-room now.*

IRINA. Masha's a bit out of sorts today. She was married at eighteen, when he seemed to her the most intelligent man in the world. It's not like that any more. He's the kindest, but not necessarily the brightest.

OLGA [*impatiently*]. Andrei, come here, we're waiting!

ANDREI [*offstage*]. Coming. [*Enters and walks to the table.*]

TUZENBACH. What are you thinking about?

IRINA. Nothing. I don't like this Solyony of yours. He frightens me. And he says such bizarre things...

TUZENBACH. He is a strange person. I pity him. He irritates me too, but I pity him more. In fact, I think he's quite shy.... When the two of us are alone together, he can be very good company, but in public he becomes rude and belligerent. Don't go, let them sit down at the table. Let me be with you for a moment. What are you thinking about?

Pause.

You're twenty, I'm not yet thirty. How many years do we have left to look forward to, a long chain of days full of my love for you...

IRINA. Nikolay, please don't talk to me about love.

TUZENBACH [*not listening*]. I have such a longing for life, for struggle, and for work and somehow this longing is mixed up with my with love for you, Irina, you're so beautiful, and life seems to me so wonderful! What are you thinking about?

IRINA. You say life is wonderful. Yes, but how can I believe it! We three sisters have not had a wonderful life so far, life has choked us like weeds.... Now the tears have started.... I don't need that... [*She wipes her face quickly and smiles.*] We need to work, to work. We're

31

unhappy and life seems bleak to us because we don't work. We were born of people who despised work...

Enter NATALYA IVANOVA*; she wears a pink dress with a green belt.*

NATASHA. Oh no! They're already sitting down for lunch ... I'm late... [*Looks in the mirror hastily, straightens up.*] At least my hair looks all right... [*noticing* IRINA]. Irina, sweetie, congratulations! [*She gives her a vigorous and long kiss.*] You have so many guests, I feel kind of shy.... Hello, Baron!

OLGA [*entering the living-room*]. Oh, here's Natasha now! How are you, my dear!

They kiss each other.

NATASHA. Congratulations. You have such a lot of people here, I'm so embarrassed...

OLGA. Don't worry, they're all close friends. [*In an undertone, alarmed.*] My dear, you're wearing a green belt! It's wrong!

NATASHA. Why, is it bad luck?

OLGA. No, it's just not the right shade ... it clashes...

NATASHA [*in a tearful voice*]. Does it? But it's not really green, it's more like beige. [*She follows* OLGA *to the dining-room.*]

32

ACT I

Everyone is in the dining-room, sitting down for lunch, there is nobody in the living-room.

KULYGIN. Irina, I wish you a fine husband. It's time you got married.

CHEBUTYKIN. Natasha, I wish you a handsome husband too.

KULYGIN. Natasha already has a fiancé.

MASHA [*taps on her plate with a fork*]. Let's have some wine, damnit! We only live once.

KULYGIN. Masha! C-minus for conduct.

VERSHININ. This cordial is delicious. What's it made of?

SOLYONY. Cockroaches.

IRINA [*tearfully*]. Ugh! How disgusting!...

OLGA. We're having roast turkey and apple pie. I'm at home the whole day, thank God, and this evening too – home.... Gentlemen, I do hope you'll join us this evening...

VERSHININ. May I come too?

IRINA. Please do.

NATASHA. It's really casual here.

CHEBUTYKIN. "Sweet is the Budding Spring of love!" [*Laughs.*]

ANDREI [*angrily*]. Stop it! Haven't you had enough?

> *Enter* FEDOTIK *and* ROHDE *with a big basket of flowers.*

FEDOTIK. Look, they're sitting down already.

ROHDE [*loudly and pronouncing r's in the French manner*]. Sitting down? You're right...

FEDOTIK. Wait a second! [*Takes a photograph.*] One! Hold on... [*Takes another photograph.*] Two! Done!

> *They take the basket and go into the dining-room, where they are greeted noisily.*

ROHDE [*loudly*]. Many happy returns! I wish you the most of everything! The weather is charming today, simply splendiferous. I spent all morning walking with the high-school students. I coach gymnastics there.

FEDOTIK. You can move now, Irina, go ahead! [*Taking a photograph.*] You look ravishing today. [*He takes a humming-top out of his pocket.*] Look, here is a little humming-top.... Listen to the sound it makes...

IRINA. Oh, how sweet!

MASHA. "Beside the sea a green oak's standing/ and on it hangs a golden chain" ... "and on it hangs a golden chain"... [*Tearfully.*] Why am I saying that anyway? I've had those words in my head since morning...

KULYGIN. Thirteen at the table!

ROHDE [*loudly*]. You don't believe those old superstitions, do you?

Laughter.

KULYGIN. If there are thirteen people at the table, it means that someone's in love. Is it you, doctor?

Laughter.

CHEBUTYKIN. I'm an old sinner, but why Natasha is turning red, I can't understand.

Loud laughter; NATASHA *runs away from the dining-room into the living-room,* ANDREI *follows her.*

ANDREI. Don't mind them! Wait, please, don't run away...

NATASHA. I'm so ashamed.... I don't know what's wrong, they're all making fun of me. I know that leaving the table like that is bad manners, but I just can't ... can't... [*covers her face with her hands*].

ANDREI. My darling, please, I beg you, don't let it bother you. I promise you, they're just having fun, they don't mean any harm. My darling, you're such a good person, they're all kind, warm people, and they love me and you. Come over by the window, they can't see us from there... [*looks around*].

NATASHA. I am not used to being in society!…

ANDREI. Oh, you're so young, so beautiful! My dearest don't worry so much!… Believe me, trust me…. I am so happy, my heart is full of love, it's overflowing…. Oh, they don't see us! I promise! Why, oh why did I fall in love with you, when did I fall in love – oh, I don't understand anything. My dearest, my love, such innocence, be my wife! I love you, I love you … as I never loved anyone before… [*They kiss.*]

> *Two* OFFICERS *come in and, seeing the two kissing, stop in amazement.*

CURTAIN

ACT II

*The set as in Act I. It is eight o'clock at night. The
room is in darkness. Outside, in the street, faint
sounds of an accordion being played.* NATASHA *enters wearing a dressing-gown, holding a candle;
she stops at the door which leads to* ANDREI*'s room.*

NATASHA. Andryusha, what are you doing? Reading? No, nothing, I just... [*Walks over, opens
another door and after looking through it,
closes it.*] No lights burning in there...

ANDREI [*comes in, with a book in his hand*]. What
is it, Natasha?

NATASHA. I'm looking to see if there's a light burning anywhere.... It's carnival week and the
servants are running wild. You need to keep
a sharp eye out. Last night around midnight,
I go into the dining-room, and what do I see?
A candle burning. Who lit it? No one's talking. [*Puts the candle on the table.*] What time
is it?

ANDREI [*looking at his watch*]. Quarter past eight.

NATASHA. And Olga and Irina not home yet. Still
hard at work, poor things. Olga at the fa-
culty meeting, Irina at the telegraph office...

[*Sighs.*] This morning I said to your sister: "You should take better care of yourself, Irina, darling." But she never listens. Quarter past eight, did you say? I'm worried, our Bobik isn't well. Why does he feel so cold? Yesterday he had a fever, but today he's cold all over.... It scares me.

ANDREI. It's all right, Natasha. The little fella is fine.

NATASHA. But still, we should watch what he eats. I do worry, I can't help it. And at ten o'clock, they say, the mummers are coming; I wish they weren't, Andrei dear.

ANDREI. I don't know anything about it. Anyway, I think they've already been invited.

NATASHA. This morning when our little boy woke up he looked up at me, and suddenly he broke into a big smile: he knows me! "Good morning Bobik!", I said, "Good morning, sweetie-pie," and he laughed. They understand, you know, babies understand everything. So, anyway, Andryusha, I'll tell them not to let the mummers in.

ANDREI [*indecisively*]. It's really up to my sisters. It is their house.

NATASHA. It's their house too. I'll let them know. They're so nice... [*She walks.*] I ordered some yoghurt for supper. The doctor says, you need to eat only yoghurt, otherwise you won't lose any weight. [*Stops.*] Bobik is so cold. I'm worried that his room is too cold. We should move him into another room, at least until the weather gets warm. Irina's room, for instance, is perfect for a baby: it's dry and it gets the sun all day long. I'll talk to her, she can share a room with Olga for now…. Irina's not here during the day anyway, she only comes home to sleep… [*Pause.*] Andrei my pet, why don't you say something?

ANDREI. Oh, I was just thinking…. Anyway, there's nothing to say.

NATASHA. Yes…. Something I meant to tell you…. Oh yes, Ferapont's here from the Council, he is asking for you.

ANDREI [*yawning*]. Send him in. [NATASHA *exits, * ANDREI *reads his book, bending over the candle she has left.* FERAPONT *comes in; he is wearing an old, worn-out coat with the collar turned up, his ears are covered.*] Evening, old-timer. What's the news?

FERAPONT. The chairman has sent you a book and some kind of letter. Here… [*gives him the book and the letter*].

ANDREI. Thanks. Yes, all right. But why are you here so late? It's after eight o'clock.

FERAPONT. What?

ANDREI [*louder*]. I say, you're late, it's after eight o'clock.

FERAPONT. That's right. When I got here it was still light, but they wouldn't let me in. The master is busy, they said. Sure, sure. If he's busy he's busy, I'm not in any hurry. [*Thinking that* ANDREI *is asking something.*] What's that?

ANDREI. Nothing. [*Looking at the book.*] Tomorrow is Friday, there's no meeting, but I'll go in anyway ... do something. It's boring at home...

    Pause.

My friend, it's a funny thing how life can shift, play tricks on you. Today, just out of boredom, nothing else to do, I took down this book – my old lecture notes from university, and I just had to laugh.... My God, I am the *secretary* of the District Council, the Council where Protopopov is the chairman, I am the secretary, and the most I can aspire to is to be a member of the Council! A member of the District Council! I, who dream every night of being a professor at the University of Moscow, the famous academic, the pride of Russia.

FERAPONT. Not quite sure, sir.... Don't hear too well...

40

Act II

ANDREI. If you could I probably wouldn't be saying all this. I have to talk to someone, but my wife doesn't understand me, and I'm strangely afraid of my sisters, afraid that they'll laugh at me, make me feel ashamed.... I don't drink, I don't like bars, but my God! What I'd give to be sitting right now in the Bolshoi Moscovskaya, or Tyestov's in Moscow. Yes, indeed.

FERAPONT. Moscow you say? This fellow at the Council the other day – a contractor – he was telling me about some merchants in Moscow who were eating pancakes; and one of them ate forty pancakes and died. Was it forty or fifty? Something like that.

ANDREI. In a Moscow restaurant, you sit in this huge dining-room, you don't know a soul, and nobody knows you, and yet you don't feel like an outsider. Whereas here you know everyone, and everyone knows you, but you're still an outsider. An outsider. And alone.

FERAPONT. What's that? [*Pause.*] And the other thing this contractor told me – mind you he could be pulling my leg – was that there is a rope stretched across the whole of Moscow.

ANDREI. A what?

FERAPONT. A rope.

ANDREI. What for?

FERAPONT. No idea. It's just what the contractor said.

ANDREI. Ridiculous. [*Reads his book.*] Have you ever been to Moscow?

FERAPONT [*after a pause*]. Never. It wasn't in God's plan. [*Pause.*] Shall I go?

ANDREI. Yes, go. Take care.

Exit FERAPONT.

Take care. [*Reading.*] Come back tomorrow morning, and I'll have these papers for you.... Go on now...

Pause.

He's gone.... Yes, that's how it is... [*stretches and slowly walks to his room*].

Offstage a nanny is singing a lullaby. MA-SHA *and* VERSHININ *enter the room. While they talk, a servant lights a lamp and candles.*

MASHA. I don't know.

Pause.

I don't know. Habit is very powerful. For instance, after father died it took us a long time to get used to the fact that there were no orderlies in the house. But aside from habit, I think what I'm saying is just the simple truth. It may be different elsewhere, but in our town all the finest people, the best-educated and the most decent, are in the military.

VERSHININ. I'm thirsty. Is there any tea?

MASHA [*looking at her watch*]. They'll be putting it out soon. I was married off when I was barely eighteen. I'd just graduated from school and I was in awe of my husband because he was a teacher. At the time I thought he was terrifyingly intelligent and important and well-educated. Not any more, unfortunately.

VERSHININ. I see ... yes.

MASHA. I don't say this about my husband, I'm used to him now, but in general, the civilians here are appallingly rude. It's shocking to me to be around people who are so lacking in sensitivity, in gentleness and simple courtesy. When I have to spend time with my husband's colleagues, the teachers, it's sheer torture.

VERSHININ. Yes, of course.... But personally, I don't see any difference between civilians or officers, they're equally tiresome. There's nothing to distinguish them. Listen to any educated man here, civilian or officer, and you'll hear the same story: he's tired of his wife, he's tired of his house, tired of his estate, tired of his horses.... The Russian is capable of such lofty ideals, but why in real life does he fall so short of them? Why?

MASHA. Why, indeed?

VERSHININ. Why is he tired of his children, why is he tired of his wife? And why is it that his wife and kids are tired of him?

MASHA. You're in a strange mood today.

VERSHININ. Yes, probably. I haven't had any dinner today, haven't eaten anything since morning. One of my girls is sick, and when my daughters aren't well, I'm anxious, I'm consumed with guilt that they have such a mother. Oh, if you could only see her today! What a piece of work! We started fighting at seven this morning, and at nine I slammed the door and left.

Pause.

I never talk about it, and for some reason, I complain only to you. [*Kisses her hand.*] Don't be angry with me. I have no one in the world but you, no one...

Pause.

MASHA. What a noise the wind's making. Just before father died, the wind was howling in the stove. The same as now.

VERSHININ. Are you superstitious?

MASHA. Yes.

VERSHININ. That's strange. [*Kisses her hand.*] You wonderful, amazing woman. Wonderful, amazing! It's dark here, but I can see your eyes shining.

MASHA [*sits down on another chair*]. There's more light here...

VERSHININ. I love, I love, I love ... I love your eyes, the way you move.... I see you in my dreams.... Wonderful, amazing woman!

MASHA [*laughing softly*]. When you speak to me like that, I can't help laughing even though it frightens me. Don't do it any more, please... [*In an undertone.*] Or ... rather ... do, I don't care... [*covers her face with her hands*]. I don't care. Someone's coming, talk about something else...

IRINA *and* TUZENBACH *come in through the dining-room.*

TUZENBACH. I have three surnames. I am Baron-Tuzenbach-Krohne-Altschauer, but I'm Russian-Orthodox, just like you. There's hardly a trace of German in me, except for this dogged determination which so annoys you. I walk you home every single night.

IRINA. I'm worn out!

TUZENBACH. And I'm going to keep coming to the telegraph office and walking you home for ten, twenty years, until you tell me to go away... [*Noticing* MASHA *and* VERSHININ, *happily.*] Oh, it's you! Good evening!

IRINA. I'm home, at last. [*To* MASHA.] A woman came in, just as I was about to leave. She wanted to send a telegram to her brother in Saratov, telling him that her son had died today, but she couldn't remember her brother's address. So she ended up just sending it to Saratov: that's all, no number, no street name. She was crying and I snapped at her for no reason. I said, "Oh, hurry up, would you." It was so stupid. Are the mummers coming tonight?

MASHA. Yes.

IRINA [*sits down in an armchair*]. I have to sit down. I'm so tired.

TUZENBACH [*smiling*]. When you come back from work, you look so young and so forlorn... [*Pause.*]

IRINA. Tired. No, I don't like the telegraph office, I don't.

MASHA. You've lost weight... [*whistling*]. And you look younger, your face looks like a boy's...

TUZENBACH. That's because of the haircut.

ACT II

IRINA. I must look for another job, this one doesn't feel right. What I wanted, what I dreamed about, that's exactly what this job doesn't have. Work without poetry, without thought...

A knocking on the floor.

The doctor is knocking. [*To* TUZENBACH.] Would you knock for me, my dear.... I can't.... I'm so tired...

TUZENBACH *knocks back.*

He'll be here in a moment. We need to discuss something. Yesterday the doctor and Andrei were at the club, and they lost at cards again. I heard that Andrei lost two hundred roubles.

MASHA [*indifferently*]. Oh well!

IRINA. He lost money two weeks ago, he lost in December. I wish he would just lose it all, then maybe we'd get out of this town. Dear God, I dream about Moscow every single night. I feel like I'm losing my mind. [*Laughs.*] We're moving there in June, but there's still February, March, April and May ... almost half a year!

MASHA. We can't let Natasha know about the money.

IRINA. I don't think she really cares.

CHEBUTYKIN comes into the room. He had a nap after a dinner and has just woken up. He combs his beard, then sits down at the table and takes a newspaper out of his pocket.

MASHA. There he is.... Has he paid his rent yet?

IRINA [*laughs*]. No. Not a kopeck in eight months. He's obviously forgotten.

MASHA [*laughs*]. Look at him, sitting there so full of himself!

Everyone is laughing; pause.

IRINA. Why are you so quiet, Aleksandr?

VERSHININ. I don't know. I need some tea. My kingdom for a cup of tea! I've had nothing to eat since this morning...

CHEBUTYKIN. Irina!

IRINA. What is it?

CHEBUTYKIN. Over here, please. *Venez ici.*

> IRINA *walks over and sits down at the table.*

I can't manage without you.

> IRINA *lays out the cards for patience.*

VERSHININ. Oh well. Since they're not giving us any tea, we might as well philosophize.

Act II

TUZENBACH. Yes, let's. What about?

VERSHININ. What about? Let us dream ... about the life to come, in two or three hundred years.

TUZENBACH. Yes. All right: in two or three hundred years, people will be flying around in balloons, men's jackets will be cut differently, scientists will have discovered a sixth sense, but life itself will be essentially the same: difficult, mysterious, and happy. And in a thousand years human beings will still be sighing and saying: "Ah, Life is so hard!" – and they'll still be just as afraid of death and make every effort to avoid it.

VERSHININ [*after a moment of thinking*]. How shall I put this? I want to get it right. I think that everything on earth is changing, little by little, but we can already see the change beginning. In two or three hundred, even a thousand years – the time doesn't matter – a new life, a happy life, will finally arrive. We won't be around to see it, of course, but we're living for it now, we are working and, well ... suffering for it, creating it – that is the meaning and purpose of our existence. That, you might say, is our happiness.

MASHA *laughs softly.*

TUZENBACH. What's so funny?

MASHA. I don't know. I've been laughing all day, since this morning.

VERSHININ. I graduated from the same school as you, but I didn't go to the Military College. I read a lot, but I don't always know what books to pick up, and probably I waste my time with useless stuff, but the longer I live, the more I want to know. My hair's turning grey, I'm not young any more, and yet how little I understand, how very little! But one thing I have learned, one thing I'm sure of. And how I wish I could make you see that real happiness isn't possible. There can't and won't be any for us in this lifetime.... But still we must work and work, and happiness – that belongs to generations yet to come.

Pause.

Happiness is not for me, but for my children's children.

FEDOTIK *and* ROHDE *appear in the dining-room; they sit down and sing quietly playing the guitar.*

TUZENBACH. So according to you, we shouldn't even dream of being happy. But what if I am!

VERSHININ. What?

TUZENBACH. Happy!

Vershinin. You're not.

Tuzenbach [*clasping his hands and laughing*]. Obviously, we're not communicating. How can I persuade you?

Masha *laughs softly.*

[*pointing at her*] Laugh! [*To* Vershinin.] Never mind two or three hundred years, in a *million* years life will be no different; it doesn't change, it remains the same, following its own immutable laws, which don't concern us, which we'll never understand. Think of migratory birds – cranes, for example. There they go, flying back and forth, winter and summer, back and forth and no matter what little thoughts, or even big thoughts might occur to them – they keep on flying and they don't know why. And if philosophers should appear among them, well, that won't stop them; let them philosophize all they want so long as they keep on flying.

Masha. But, there must be some meaning to it all?

Tuzenbach. The meaning.... Look, it's snowing. What's the meaning?

Pause.

Masha. I think, a person either has to believe in something or else be searching for something to believe in, otherwise his life is empty, just empty.... To live and not know why cranes fly south, why children are born, why there are stars in the sky ... either you know what you're living for, or everything is meaningless, a waste...

Pause.

VERSHININ. Still, it's a pity not to be young any more.

MASHA. As Gogol said: it's a bore living on this earth, my friends.

TUZENBACH. Well, I'd say it's a chore arguing with you, my friends! I give up...

CHEBUTYKIN [*reading a newspaper*]. Balzac was married in Berdichev.

IRINA *sings quietly.*

Better write that down in my book. [*Writes it down.*] Balzac was married in Berdichev. [*Reads the newspaper.*]

IRINA [*lays out cards for patience, deep in thought*]. Balzac was married in Berdichev.

TUZENBACH. The die is cast. You know I'm handing in my resignation.

MASHA. So I heard. And I don't see anything good in that. I don't like civilians...

TUZENBACH. Ah well, too bad... [*Gets up.*] I'm not

handsome, what sort of figure do I cut as an officer? Well, anyway, what's the difference.... I'm going to work. If just for one day in my life, I want to work to the point of exhaustion. I want to come home at night, collapse into bed and drop off instantly. [*Exiting to the dining-room.*] People who work must sleep so well!

FEDOTIK [*to* IRINA]. I got these coloured pencils for you just now, at Pyzhikovs' in Moscow Street. And this little sharpener too...

IRINA. You still treat me like a child, but I'm all grown up, you know. [*Takes the pencils and the knife, happily.*] Oh, how lovely!

FEDOTIK. And for myself, I bought a penknife ... take a look ... here's a blade and here's another one, and a third, and this is to clean your ears, this is a little pair of scissors, and this one's for your nails...

ROHDE [*loudly*]. Doctor, how old are you?

CHEBUTYKIN. Me? I'm thirty-two.

Laughter.

FEDOTIK. I'll show you another kind of patience now... [*Lays out cards for patience.*]

> *The samovar is brought out;* ANFISA *looks after it. In a moment,* NATASHA *comes in and also helps at the table;* SOLYONY *comes in and saying hello, sits down at the table.*

VERSHININ. My, what a wind, though!

MASHA. Yes. I'm fed up with winter. I've almost forgotten what summer is like.

IRINA. The cards are going to turn out right, I see. We will get to Moscow.

FEDOTIK. No they're not. Look, the eight turned up on the two of spades. [*Laughs.*] It means you won't get to Moscow.

CHEBUTYKIN [*reads a newspaper*]. Zizikar. Small-pox is raging there.

ANFISA [*approaching* MASHA]. Masha, have some tea, dear. [*To* VERSHININ.] You too, Excellency … I'm sorry, love, I've forgotten your name…

MASHA. Bring it over here, nanny. I'm not going over there.

IRINA. Nana!

ANFISA. Com-ing!

NATASHA [*to* SOLYONY]. They understand every-thing, babies. I said, "Good morning, Bobik. Good morning, sweetie-pie!" And he gave this *look*. I know, you think it's just the mother in me speaking, but no, believe me! He is a most unusual baby.

SOLYONY. If that baby were mine, I'd fry him in a frying-pan and eat him. [*Goes to the living-room with a glass in his hand and sits down in the corner.*]

Act II

NATASHA [*burying her face in her hands*]. Oh, what a horrible, rude man!

MASHA. Happy the man who doesn't care whether it's summer or winter. I think, if I were living in Moscow, I wouldn't pay any attention to the weather...

VERSHININ. I've been reading the diaries of this French cabinet minister, written when he was in prison. He played some role in the Panama affair. With what intense joy he writes about the birds he sees through his prison window, which he doesn't remember seeing when he was in office. Now that he's free, of course, he won't notice them any more. In the same way, you won't notice Moscow when you're living there. We aren't happy and we can't be happy, we just long to be so.

TUZENBACH [*takes a box from the table*]. Where are the chocolates?

IRINA. Solyony ate them.

TUZENBACH. What, all of them?

ANFISA [*serving tea*]. A note for you, sir.

VERSHININ. For me? [*Takes the letter.*] It's from my daughter. [*Reads it.*] Yes, of course... [*to* MASHA] Excuse me. I'll just slip out quietly. I won't have any tea. [*Gets up, agitated.*] The same old story...

MASHA. What's the matter? Is it a secret?

VERSHININ [*in a low voice*]. My wife has poisoned herself again. I have to go. I'll slip out so no one will notice. It's all so sordid. [*Kisses* MASHA's *hand.*] My dear, my good, kind woman.... I'll just slip out this way... [*Exit.*]

ANFISA. Where on Earth is he going? And I've just served him tea.... What a huffy-puffy.

MASHA [*losing her temper*]. Leave me alone! You're always fussing, I never get any peace... [*Walks with her cup towards the table.*] I've had enough of you, you old fusspot!

ANFISA. What's got into you, Mashenka?

ANDREI*'s voice offstage: "Anfisa!"*

ANFISA [*mimicking him*]. Anfisa! Just sitting in there... [*Exit.*]

MASHA [*in the dining-room, at the table, angrily*]. Let me sit down, would you! [*Mixes up the cards on the table.*] Sitting around with your cards all over the place. Drink your tea!

IRINA. You're so mean, Mashka.

MASHA. If I'm mean, don't talk to me. Don't touch me!

CHEBUTYKIN [*laughing*]. Don't touch her, don't touch...

Act II

MASHA. You're sixty, but you act like you're still a teenager, always jabbering the hell knows what.

NATASHA [*sighs*]. Masha, dear, must you talk that way? You know, to be perfectly honest, with your good looks you could be really charming company, if it weren't for your language. *Je vous prie pardonnez moi, Marie, mais vous avez des manières un peu grossières...*

TUZENBACH [*holding back laughter*]. Would you ... would you ... over there, I think there's some cognac.

NATASHA. *Il paraît que mon Bobik déjà ne dort pas*, he's awake. He isn't well today. I'll just go check on him, excuse me... [*Exit.*]

IRINA. Where's Vershinin?

MASHA. Home. Some dreadful business with his wife.

TUZENBACH [*walks to* SOLYONY, *a decanter of cognac in his hands*]. You're always sitting alone, brooding – about what, for God's sake? Come on, let's call a truce. Have some cognac.

They drink.

I'll probably have to play the piano all night, all kinds of rubbish ... ah, well.

SOLYONY. Why should we call a truce? We don't have a problem.

TUZENBACH. I always feel that there's something's wrong between us. You're a strange duck, you know.

SOLYONY [*reciting*]. "I am strange, but who's not strange? Be not wroth, Aleko!"

TUZENBACH. What's Aleko got to do with it… [*Pause.*]

SOLYONY. When I'm just talking one on one I'm fine, I can be quite normal, but in a group I get nervous, I feel shy … and then I say stupid things. Still, I'm more honest and more ethical than a lot of people. You'll see, one day.

TUZENBACH. It gets on my nerves the way you pester me when others are around, yet for some reason I like you. Okay, I'm going to get drunk. Let's drink!

SOLYONY. Let's drink.

They drink.

I've never had anything against you, Baron. But I've got something of Lermontov's temperament. [*Quietly.*] I even look a bit like him … so I've been told… [*He takes a bottle of perfume from his pocket and pours some on his hands.*]

TUZENBACH. I'm handing in my resignation. Enough is enough! For five years, I've been thinking about it, and finally, I've made up my mind. I'm going to work.

SOLYONY [*reciting*]. "Be not wroth, Aleko.... Forget, forget your dreams..."

> *While they are talking,* ANDREI *walks in quietly with a book and sits down by the candle.*

TUZENBACH. At last, finally, I'm going to work...

CHEBUTYKIN [*walking into the living-room with* IRINA]. And there was real Caucasian food too: onion soup, and for the meat course – *chekhartma.*

SOLYONY. *Cheremsha* isn't meat; it's a vegetable like an onion.

CHEBUTYKIN. No, my angel. *Chekhartma* is not onion, it's lamb stew.

SOLYONY. But I'm telling you that *cheremsha* is an onion.

CHEBUTYKIN. And I'm telling you that *chekhartma* is lamb.

SOLYONY. And I'm telling you that *cheremsha* is onion.

CHEBUTYKIN. What's the use of arguing with you. You've never been to the Caucasus and you've never eaten *chekhartma.*

SOLYONY. I haven't eaten it because I can't stand it. *Cheremsha* smells exactly like garlic.

ANDREI [*imploring*]. That's enough, gentlemen! I beg you!

TUZENBACH. When are the mummers coming?

IRINA. They promised to be here by nine; so any minute now.

TUZENBACH [*hugging* ANDREI]. *Oh my porch, my porch, my new maple porch...*

ANDREI [*dancing and singing*]. *My new maple porch...*

CHEBUTYKIN [*dancing*]. *My porch with a lattice on the door!*

Laughter.

TUZENBACH [*kisses* ANDREI]. Hey, Andryusha, to hell with it all! A toast to friendship! Let's go to Moscow together, Andryusha, let's go back to university.

SOLYONY. Which one? There are two universities in Moscow.

ANDREI. Actually, there's only one university in Moscow.

SOLYONY. But I'm telling you, there's two.

ANDREI. There's three, whatever. Even better.

SOLYONY. There are two universities in Moscow!

Murmurs of disapproval and hushing.

There are two universities in Moscow: the old one and the new one. But if you don't want to listen to me, if my conversation is so extremely irksome to you, I can stop talking. I'll even go to another room... [*Goes out through one of the doors.*]

TUZENBACH. Bravo, bravo! [*Laughs.*] My friends, I am sitting down at the piano, let the festivities begin! He's a funny fellow, that Solyony... [*Sits down at the piano, plays a waltz.*]

MASHA [*waltzing alone*]. The Baron's drunk, the Baron's drunk, the Baron's drunk!

Enter NATASHA.

NATASHA [*to* CHEBUTYKIN]. Doctor! [*She says something to* CHEBUTYKIN, *then goes out quietly.*]

CHEBUTYKIN *touches* TUZENBACH*'s shoulder and whispers something to him.*

IRINA. What's the matter?

CHEBUTYKIN. It's time we were going. Take care.

TUZENBACH. Good night. Time to go.

IRINA. Wait a minute.... What about the mummers?

ANDREI [*embarrassed*]. We aren't having the mummers. You know, Natasha says Bobik's not well, and so she thought.... To be honest, I don't even know, it makes no difference to me.

IRINA [*shrugging her shoulders*]. If Bobik's not well!

MASHA. Oh, hell! They're kicking us out, so we have to go. [*To* IRINA.] It's not Bobik who's not well, it's her.... Here! [*taps on her forehead*] Stupid little bourgeoise!

> ANDREI *exits to his room through the door on the right,* CHEBUTYKIN *follows him; sounds of good-bye in the dining-room.*

FEDOTIK. That's a shame! I was counting on spending a nice evening here, but if the little one's sick, then, of course.... I'll bring him some toys tomorrow...

ROHDE [*loudly*]. I had a good nap after dinner on purpose, I thought I was going to dance all night. It's only nine o'clock!

MASHA. Let's go outside and have a talk there. We'll figure something out.

> *Sound of "Good-bye! Take care!".* TUZEN-BACH *is heard laughing happily. Everybody leaves.* ANFISA *with a maid clears the table and puts out the lights. A nanny is heard singing.* ANDREI, *wearing an overcoat and a hat, and* CHEBUTYKIN *walk in quietly.*

CHEBUTYKIN. I never had time to get married, because my life went by like a flash of lightning, and also I was passionately in love with your mother and she was married...

ANDREI. Don't get married. It's boring.

CHEBUTYKIN. That may be, but the loneliness. Whatever you may say, loneliness is a frightening thing, my boy.... But anyway ... it doesn't matter.

ANDREI. Let's hurry.

CHEBUTYKIN. Why? There's lots of time.

ANDREI. I'm afraid my wife might stop us.

CHEBUTYKIN. Ah!

ANDREI. I won't play today, I'll just sit there.... I don't feel well. I can't catch my breath. What should I do, doctor?

CHEBUTYKIN. Don't ask me! I don't remember any of it, my boy. Not a damn thing.

ANDREI. Let's go through the kitchen. [*They exit.*]

The sound of a bell, then again; sounds of voices, laughter.

IRINA [*enter*]. Who's that?

ANFISA [*whispering*]. The mummers!

Bell.

IRINA. Tell them there's nobody home, Nana. Apologize to them.

ANFISA *exits.* IRINA *walks about thinking; she is agitated. Enter* SOLYONY.

SOLYONY [*perplexed*]. Nobody here ... where did they all go?

IRINA. Home.

SOLYONY. That's strange. You're here alone?

IRINA. Yes. All alone.

Pause.

Good-bye.

SOLYONY. I was rude just now, and I lost my self-control. But you're not like the others, you're so much finer, so much purer, and you see the truth.... You're the only person who can understand me. I love you, I love you – profoundly, eternally.

IRINA. No, no. Good-bye! Go away. Please.

SOLYONY. I can't live without you. [*Following her.*] My bliss! [*through tears*] Oh, such happiness! Beautiful, wonderful, magnificent eyes, eyes like no other woman's.

IRINA [*coldly*]. Stop it! Stop it!

SOLYONY. It's the first time I've ever spoken of my love, and I feel as if I weren't even on the same planet as you. [*Rubs his forehead.*] Well, it doesn't make any difference. I can't make you love me, of course.... But I won't

stand for any rivals.... No rivals.... I swear
by all that's holy, I'll kill anyone who tries
to.... Oh, wonderful one!

NATASHA *passes by with a candle.*

NATASHA [*looks into one door, then into another,
walks past the door leading to her husband's
room*]. There's Andrei. That's fine. He can
go on reading. [*To* SOLYONY.] Oh! Excuse me,
won't you? I didn't know you were here, I'm
not quite dressed...

SOLYONY. What the hell do I care? Good-bye! [*Exit.*]

NATASHA. Look at you, you're so tired, my dear,
poor little girl! [*Kisses* IRINA.] You'd better
go to bed early.

IRINA. Is Bobik asleep?

NATASHA. Asleep. For now. By the way, dear, I've
been meaning to tell you, but you're either
out or I'm too busy.... Bobik's room is really
too cold and damp for him, I think. Your
room is perfect for a child. Darling one, could
you move in with Olya for a while?

IRINA [*not understanding*]. Move in where?

*Sounds of a troika with bells approaching
the house.*

NATASHA. You'll be in a room with Olya for a while,
and Bobik can have your room. He is so *cute*,
today I said to him: "Bobik, you're mine! All

mine!" And he just looked up at me with those bright little eyes.

Bell.

That must be Olga. She's so late!

MAID *comes up to* NATASHA *and whispers something in her ear.*

NATASHA. Protopopov? What a funny man. Protopopov's here, asking me out for a ride in his troika. [*Laughs.*] Men! They're so crazy!...

Bell.

Someone else is at the door. I suppose I could go for fifteen minutes... [*To the* MAID.] Tell him, I'll be down in a moment.

Bell.

Someone's ringing ... that must be Olga... [*Exit.*]

The MAID *hurries away;* IRINA *sits deep in thought; enter* KULYGIN, OLGA, *followed by* VERSHININ.

KULYGIN. That's a surprise. They said they were having a party.

VERSHININ. Strange, when I left half an hour ago they were waiting for the mummers to arrive...

IRINA. Everybody's gone.

KULYGIN. Masha too? Where did she go? And why is Protopopov waiting downstairs in his troika? Who is he waiting for?

IRINA. Don't ask questions ... I'm tired.

KULYGIN. Spoiled little girl...

OLGA. The meeting just finished. I'm exhausted. Our headmistress is sick, so I have to fill in. My head is pounding, oh my head, my head... [*Sits down.*] Andrei lost two hundred roubles playing cards yesterday.... It's the talk of the town...

KULYGIN. Yes, the meeting tired me out, too. I'm pooped. [*Sits down.*]

VERSHININ. My wife decided to scare me just now, she tried to poison herself. Everything's fine however, thank goodness, I can relax.... Should we leave? Well, let me wish you all the best. Fyodor, why don't we go somewhere together! I can't go home, I can't.... Let's go somewhere!

KULYGIN. Too tired. I can't. [*Gets up.*] I am ready to drop. Has my wife gone home?

IRINA. I suppose so.

KULYGIN [*kisses* IRINA's *hand*]. Good-bye. Tomorrow and the day after tomorrow I'm just going to rest. All the best! [*Goes.*] I'd love some tea. I'd counted on spending the evening in pleasant company and – oh, *fallacem hominum spem*! Accusative case with exclamation...

VERSHININ. Well then, I'll go by myself! [*Exit with* KULYGIN, *whistling.*]

OLGA. Oh, my head, my head is pounding.... Andrei's lost ... Everyone's talking.... I'm going to lie down. [*Goes.*] Tomorrow I'm free.... My God, that's a wonderful thought! Tomorrow I'm free, the day after tomorrow I'm free.... My head is pounding, my head... [*Exit.*]

IRINA [*alone*]. Everyone's gone. Nobody here.

> *Sound of harmonica on the street, a nanny is singing.*

NATASHA. [*in a fur coat and a hat walks through the living-room; followed by a maid*]. I'll be back in half an hour. Just going for a short drive. [*Exit.*]

IRINA [*left alone, yearning*]. Moscow! To Moscow! To Moscow!

CURTAIN

ACT III

OLGA and IRINA's room. To the left and to the right are beds with screens in front of them. It is past two in the morning. There are sounds of fire bells offstage. The fire started a long time ago. It is clear that no one in the house has gone to bed. MASHA is lying on the sofa. She is wearing a black dress as usual. Enter OLGA and ANFISA.

ANFISA. They're down there right now, sitting under the stairs.... I told them, I said, "Come on now, girls, come on up, you shouldn't be sitting there" – but they just kept crying, "Daddy! Daddy! Where is he? What if he's burned to death". What an idea! And the yard full of people ... half-dressed, most of them.

OLGA [*takes some clothes out of the closet*]. Here. Take this grey dress ... and this one too ... and this blouse.... And the skirt, Nana.... What is all that, my God! All of Kirsanov Lane has burned down, apparently.... Take this.... Take this [*she tosses the clothes to ANFISA*]. The Vershinins have had a shock, poor things.... Their house nearly caught fire. They can stay the night at our place ...

69

they mustn't be allowed to go home.... Poor
Fedotik has lost everything...

ANFISA. Olyushka, call Ferapont. I can't carry it
all...

OLGA [*rings*]. No point ringing... [*Through the
door.*] Can anyone give us a hand?

> *Through the open door a window can be
> seen, red with the blaze; sounds of the fire
> brigade driving by the house.*

Oh, it's horrible! I'm so sick of it!

Enter FERAPONT.

Here, take this downstairs.... The Kolotilin
girls are sitting under the stairs ... give it
to them. And give them this as well...

FERAPONT. Yes ma'am. In 1812 it was Moscow that
was burning. Oh my, yes. And weren't the
French surprised!

OLGA. Go now, go.

FERAPONT. Yes ma'am. [*Exit.*]

OLGA. Nana sweetheart, give it all away. We don't
need anything, give it all away, nanny.... I
am so tired I can barely stand up.... We can't
let the Vershinins go home.... The girls can
sleep in the living-room, and Vershinin can
share a room with the Baron.... Fedotik can
stay with the Baron too, or else sleep in the

dining-room.... The Doctor is in a state –
he's gotten horribly drunk, so we can't put
anyone in with him. Vershinin's wife can
sleep in the living-room too.

ANFISA [*wearily*]. Olyushka, my sweet, don't send
me away! Don't send me away!

OLGA. Don't be silly, Nana. Nobody's sending you
away.

ANFISA [*puts her head on* OLGA's *breast*]. My darling, my treasure, I work hard, you know I
do.... But I'm old, I'll get feeble, and then
they'll say get out! And where can I go?
Where? At eighty years old. Nearly eighty-
one...

OLGA. Come on, sit down now, Nana.... You're tired, you poor thing... [*getting her to sit down*].
Just rest yourself, sweetheart. You look so
pale!

Enter NATASHA.

NATASHA. They're all downstairs talking about or-
ganizing a committee to help the people
whose houses were burnt. Well, I mean, of
course. It's our duty to help the poor. Bobik
and Sophochka are fast asleep as if nothing
had happened. There are so many people
everywhere, the house is full of them. And
with this flu going around, I'm afraid the
children might catch it.

OLGA [*not listening*]. You can't see the fire from this room, it's quite peaceful here...

NATASHA. Yes.... Look at me, I'm a mess. [*In front of the mirror.*] Who says I've put on weight.... It's not true! At all! And Masha's sleeping, she's worn out, poor girl... [*To* ANFISA *coldly.*] How dare you sit down in my presence! Get up! Get out!

Exit ANFISA; *pause.*

Why you keep that old woman around, I cannot understand!

OLGA [*taken aback*]. I'm sorry, I'm afraid *I* don't quite understand...

NATASHA. She's no use to anyone here. She's a peasant, she belongs out in the country.... You're just spoiling her! I like order in the house! No useless hangers-on. [*Strokes her cheek.*] You're tired, you poor thing! Our headmistress is tired! When my Sophochka gets big enough for high school, I'm going to be afraid of you.

OLGA. I won't be headmistress.

NATASHA. Olechka, of course you will. It's already been decided.

OLGA. I won't accept. I can't.... I'm not strong enough... [*drinks water*]. You were so rude to nanny just now.... I'm sorry, but I just

can't bear it.... I can't breathe and I just see
black in front of my eyes ...

NATASHA [*agitated*]. Forgive me, Olya, forgive
me.... I didn't mean to upset you.

> MASHA *gets up, takes her pillow and leaves,
> very angry.*

OLGA. Try to understand, my dear.... I know we've
had a very strange upbringing, but I just
can't bear it. It depresses me to see people
treated that way. It makes me physically
ill.... I just feel like giving up!

NATASHA. Forgive me, forgive me... [*Kisses her.*]

OLGA. Any kind of rudeness, or insensitivity, even
a tactless remark – I can't tell you how it
distresses me...

NATASHA. I know, I say things that I shouldn't,
but you must see, my dear, she should be
living in the country.

OLGA. She's been with us for thirty years!

NATASHA. But she can't work any more! Either I
don't understand you or you don't want to
understand me. She can't work. She just
sleeps or sits around all day.

OLGA. Then let her sit.

NATASHA [*surprised*]. What do you mean let her
sit? She's a servant, isn't she? [*Through her*

tears.] I don't understand you, Olya. I have
a nanny, a wet-nurse for the baby, we have
a maid, a cook ... what do we need this old
woman for? What for?

Sound of fire bells offstage.

OLGA. I've aged ten years tonight.

NATASHA. We have to come to some kind of
arrangement, Olya. You're at school, I'm at
home, you've got your teaching, I've got the
housekeeping. And if I say something about
the servants, I know what I am talking
about. I-know-what-I-am-talking-about....
And tomorrow morning this old thief, this
old wretch [*stamps her feet*], this witch is
out of here!... And don't you dare contradict
me! Don't you dare! [*Coming to her senses.*]
Really, if you don't move downstairs, we'll
be bickering like this all the time. It's just
awful.

Enter KULYGIN.

KULYGIN. Where is Masha? It's time to go home.
They say the fire is dying down. [*Stretches.*]
Only one block's gone, in spite of the wind;
at first it seemed like the whole city would
catch fire. [*Sits down.*] I'm exhausted.
Olechka my sweet ... I often think: if there
were no Masha, I would have married you,
Olechka. You are so good.... I'm worn out.
[*Tries to hear something.*]

ACT III

OLGA. What?

KULYGIN. The Doctor's been on a bender, he's a little worse for wear. Unfortunately. As if he'd done it on purpose. [*Gets up.*] There, it looks like he's coming.... Can you hear? Yes, he's coming... [*Laughs.*] He is such a ... I'm going to hide. [*Walks toward the closet and stands in the corner.*] He's a holy terror.

OLGA. He hasn't had a drop in two years, and now all of a sudden he decides to get roaring drunk... [*Goes to the far end of the room with* NATASHA.]

> *Enter* CHEBUTYKIN; *he walks across the room not staggering, as if he were sober; stops, looks, then approaches the washbasin and starts to wash his hands.*

CHEBUTYKIN [*gloomily*]. To hell with them all... goddamn it.... They think I'm a doctor, I'm supposed to know how to cure people, but I don't know a goddamn thing. Not a goddamn thing. It's all forgotten, nothing left of it.

> *Exit* OLGA *and* NATASHA *unnoticed by him.*

To hell with them. All of them ... Last Wednesday I treated a woman in Zasyp – she died, and it's all my fault. Yes ... I used to know something, about twenty-five years ago. But now it's all gone. My mind's a blank. Empty. Maybe I'm not even a human being any more. Maybe I just think I have legs,

75

hands, a head; maybe I don't really exist, and I only think that I walk, eat, sleep. [*Weeps.*] Oh, if only. If only I really didn't exist! [*Stops crying, gloomily.*] God knows.... The other day there was a conversation going on at the club – they were talking about Shakespeare, Voltaire.... I've never read any of it, not a single line, but I sat there with this expression on my face, looking as if I had. The same with the others. Disgusting! And then I thought of that woman, the one I let die ... and it all came back to me, my stomach knotted up, I wanted to retch.... So instead I got drunk...

Enter IRINA, VERSHININ *and* TUZENBACH. TUZENBACH *is wearing a new, fashionable civilian suit.*

IRINA. Let's sit down. No one will come in here.

VERSHININ. If it hadn't been for the soldiers, the whole town would have burned down. Good men! [*Rubs his hands with pleasure.*] The salt of the earth! Excellent fellows!

KULYGIN [*approaching them*]. What is the time, if you please?

TUZENBACH. Past three, already. It's getting light.

IRINA. Everyone is sitting in the dining-room, nobody's leaving. Your friend Solyony is there... [*To* CHEBUTYKIN.] You'd better go to bed, doctor.

CHEBUTYKIN. That's alright ma'am.... Many thanks, ma'am. [*Combs his beard.*]

KULYGIN [*laughs*]. You're pickled, Ivan Romanych! [*Slaps him on the shoulder.*] Good for you! *In vino veritas* – as the ancients used to say.

TUZENBACH. I've been asked to organize a concert for the victims of the fire.

IRINA. But who could you get to perform?...

TUZENBACH. It could be done, if there's a will. Masha plays the piano beautifully.

KULYGIN. Oh, yes, beautfully!

IRINA. She hasn't played for three years ... or is it four. She's forgotten how.

TUZENBACH. In this whole town there is not one person, no one who understands music – but I do and I can tell you, Masha has a rare gift, a great, great talent.

KULYGIN. You're right, Baron. I love Masha very much. She's very special.

TUZENBACH. To be able to play so brilliantly and at the same time to know that no one, not a soul understands you!

KULYGIN [*sighs*]. Yes.... But would it be appropriate for her to appear on a stage?

Pause.

Mind you, what do I know. It could be fine. Our principal, I have to say, is a good man, he's a very good man, and a superior intellect, but he does have certain – ideas and opinions.... Not that it's any of his business, but anyway, if you want, I could probably speak to him...

CHEBUTYKIN *picks up a china clock and looks at it.*

VERSHININ. I got filthy at the fire. I must look like some creature from the underworld.

Pause.

Yesterday, I caught wind that they want to transfer our brigade somewhere far away. Poland, maybe – or possibly even Siberia.

TUZENBACH. Yes, I've heard that, too. What will happen then? The town will be deserted.

IRINA. But we'll have moved too!

CHEBUTYKIN [*drops the clock, smashing it*]. Smithereens!

Pause; everyone is upset and embarrassed.

KULYGIN [*collecting pieces*]. To break such an expensive thing – ah, Ivan Romanych, Ivan Romanych! F-minus for conduct!

IRINA. That's mama's clock.

CHEBUTYKIN. What if it is, what if it is ... So it was mama's. Well, maybe I didn't break it, maybe it only seems that I've broken it. Maybe it only seems to us that we exist, but in reality we don't. I don't know, nobody knows. [*At the door.*] What are you staring at? Natasha is having it off with Protopopov, but you don't see that.... You sit here and see nothing, but Natasha is having it off with Protopopov... [*Sings.*] Would you care for a fig, mademoiselle... [*Exit.*]

VERSHININ. Yes... [*Laughs*] So strange, all of this!

Pause.

When the fire started, I ran straight home. When I got near, I could see that our house was fine, in no danger, but there on the front step in their nighties were my two girls, their mother nowhere to be seen, people rushing everywhere, horses and dogs running amok, and the look of terror on my girls' faces, the look of imploring. It wrung my heart, you know, to see those little faces looking up at me. My God, I thought, what else will these girls have to witness in their long life! I picked them up and ran, and I kept asking myself: what else will they have to witness in this world!

Fire bells; pause.

And then I get to your house, and find their mother here, screaming and shouting.

Enter MASHA *with a pillow and sits down on the sofa.*

And when I saw my little girls standing in their nighties in the doorway, the street red with fire, and filled with terrible noises, I thought it's like a scene out of history, when the enemy would attack out of nowhere, looting and pillaging, burning the houses.... And really, what is the difference between our age and any other? When a few more years have passed, two or three hundred perhaps, people will look at our age with shock and dismay, and everything about it will seem clumsy and heavy, and uncomfortable, and strange. Oh, but what a life it will be, what a life! [*Laughs.*] Excuse me, I'm getting carried away again. If you'll indulge me. I need to philosophize, I'm in that kind of mood.

Pause.

It's as if they were all asleep. So as I was saying: what a life it will be! Try and imagine it.... Right now there are only three people like you in this town, but in a few more generations there will be more, and then more and more, and then one day everyone will think as you do, and live as you do, and then eventually even your way of life will

Act III

become obsolete, and there will be people born who will be even finer than you... [*Laughs.*] I'm in a funny mood tonight. I have such a desire to live... [*Sings.*] "It's love that makes the world go round / To its service young and old are bound..." [*Laughing.*]

MASHA. Tum-ta-tum.

VERSHININ. Ta-tum...

MASHA. Tra-la-la?

VERSHININ. Tra-la-la. [*Laughs.*]

Enter FEDOTIK.

FEDOTIK [*dances*]. Burnt! Burned to ashes! All of it burnt!

Laughter.

IRINA. Fedotik, are you joking? Have you really lost everything?

FEDOTIK [*laughs*]. Every single thing. There's nothing left. The guitar, the photos, all my letters.... A heap of ashes. And I had a little notebook to give you – but it's gone.

Enter SOLYONY.

IRINA. No, please, go away. You can't come in here.

SOLYONY. Why is the Baron allowed in?

VERSHININ. We should go. What about the fire?

SOLYONY. Dying down, I gather. No, it's really interesting, why the Baron is allowed in and not me. [*Takes out a bottle of cologne and sprinkles some on his hands.*]

VERSHININ. Tum-tum-tum?

MASHA. Tum-tum.

VERSHININ [*laughs, to* SOLYONY]. Come on. Let's go into the dining-room.

SOLYONY. All right. We'll make a note of that: "This thought I further could make clear/ but the geese may get annoyed I fear..." [*Looking at* TUZENBACH.] Cheep, cheep, cheep... [*Exits together with* VERSHININ *and* FEDOTIK.]

IRINA. Solyony's fumigated the room with his cologne... [*Perplexed.*] The Baron's sleeping! Baron! Baron!

TUZENBACH [*woken up*]. Yes, but I'm so tired.... At the brickyard, you know.... No, I'm not talking in my sleep, I'm going to the brickyard soon, I'm going to start work there.... I've talked to them already. [*Tenderly to* IRINA.] You're so lovely, so pale.... Your face is glimmering in the darkness.... You're sad, life has let you down.... Come away with me, why don't you, we'll go away together and we'll work!

MASHA. Nikolai, go home.

TUZENBACH [*laughing*]. Oh, you're here, are you? I can't see anything. [*Kisses* IRINA's *hand.*] Good-bye, I must go.... Looking at you just now, I had a sudden image of you on your name day party, such a long time ago. You were so radiant that day, so full of joy. You spoke about work with such passion.... What a life I imagined back then! Where is it? [*Kisses her hand.*] You've got tears in your eyes. Go to bed, it's getting light ... it's almost morning.... If only you would let me give my whole life for you!

MASHA. Nikolai, go away! Seriously, now.

TUZENBACH. I'm going... [*Exit.*]

MASHA [*lying down*]. Are you asleep, Fyodor?

KULYGIN. Eh?

MASHA. Go home, why don't you.

KULYGIN. Masha darling, my dear Masha...

IRINA. She's tired. She needs to rest, Fedya.

KULYGIN. I'll go in a minute.... My good, my wonderful wife.... I love you, my only one...

MASHA [*angrily*]. *Amo, amas, amat, amamus, amatis, amant.*

KULYGIN [*laughs*]. No, listen, she really is amazing. We were married seven years ago, but it seems like only yesterday. Swear to God.

You are an amazing woman. I'm content, I'm content, I'm content!

MASHA. And I'm bored, bored, bored. [*Sits up and speaks while sitting.*] And this, it's driving me crazy.... It's so outrageous. *I can't keep quiet.* It's like a nail being pounded into my head. I'm talking about Andrei.... He's mortgaged this house to the bank and his wife's got hold of all the money, but the house doesn't belong to him alone, it belongs to all four of us! He must know it, if he has any decency.

KULYGIN. Why let it get to you, Masha? What's the difference! Andrei owes money to everyone, just leave him alone!

MASHA. I'm just saying that it's outrageous. [*Lies down.*]

KULYGIN. We're not poor. I work, I teach at school, then I tutor.... I'm a plain, honest man.... *Omnia mea mecum porto*, as they say...

MASHA. I don't want anything, but I can't bear injustice.

Pause.

Go, Fyodor.

KULYGIN [*kisses her*]. You're tired, rest for a half an hour. I'll sit up and wait for you. Sleep... [*walks*]. I'm content, I'm content, I'm content. [*Exits.*]

ACT III

IRINA. Yes, Andrei has really gone downhill, living with that woman. He's become petty, and dull and middle-aged. Once he was aiming to be a professor, but yesterday he was bragging that he'd finally been made a member of the District Council. He's a member of the Council, and Protopopov is the chairman.... The whole town is talking about it, laughing up their sleeves, he's the only one who doesn't know anything and doesn't see.... And tonight while everyone else has run off to fight the fire, he's been sitting in his room oblivious to it all. Just playing his violin... [*Agitated.*] Oh, it's awful, awful, awful! [*Weeps.*] I can't, I can't bear any more!... I can't, I can't!...

Enter OLGA, *tidies up her dressing table.*

[*Sobs loudly.*] Throw me away, throw me away, I can't stand any more!...

OLGA [*frightened*]. What is it, what is it? My darling!

IRINA [*sobbing*]. Where is it? Where's it all gone? Oh God, God! I've forgotten it all, everything.... It's all mixed up in my head.... I don't remember the Italian for *window*, or *ceiling*.... I am forgetting it all, every single day, and life is passing us by and it will never come back, never, and we'll never get to Moscow.... I see that now, we won't...

OLGA. My darling, my darling...

IRINA [*collecting herself*]. Oh, I'm so miserable....
I can't work, I won't work. Enough, enough!
I worked at the telegraph office, now I work
for the town council, and I hate and despise
everything about it.... I'm nearly twenty-
four, I've been working all this time and my
brain is drying up, I've gotten thin, and old
and ugly, and nothing, nothing, no satisfaction, and time is passing and it seems that
we're getting farther and farther away from
the real life, the beautiful life, farther and
farther away, and I feel like I'm falling into
a pit of darkness. I'm in despair, and how it
is I'm still alive, how it is I haven't killed
myself yet, I don't understand...

OLGA. Don't cry, my little girl, don't cry.... It hurts
me...

IRINA. I am not crying, I'm not.... Enough.... See,
I am not crying any more. Enough....
Enough!

OLGA. Dear little girl, my sweet girl, I'm going to
say something to you as your sister, and your
friend. Take my advice, and marry the
Baron!

IRINA *is crying quietly.*

You respect him, don't you? You value
him?... I know, he's not attractive, but he's

86

a decent man, and a good person. And anyway, people don't marry out of love, but to fulfil their duty. That's what I believe, anyway, and I would marry without love. Whoever would ask me, I would marry him, as long as he was a decent man. Even an old man, I'd marry him...

IRINA. I've been waiting all this time, thinking we'd move to Moscow, and I'd meet my true love there, I dreamed of him, I was in love with him.... But it turned out to be nonsense, just nonsense...

OLGA [*hugs her sister*]. Oh, my beautiful girl, I do understand, I do; when the Baron left the army and showed up on our doorstep in a suit, he looked so homely, I actually started to cry.... He said to me, "Why are you crying?" What could I say! But if it were God's will that he should marry you, I would be very happy. Because that would be different, completely different.

NATASHA *crosses the stage with a candle without saying a word.*

MASHA [*sits up*]. She walks around as if she'd started the fire.

OLGA. Masha, you are a silly. You know who's the silliest in our family? It's you. I'm sorry.

Pause.

MASHA. Oh, my dear sisters, I want to confess something to you. My soul is in torment. I'll confess it to you and then never again to anyone else.... I'm going to say it now, this minute. [*In a low voice.*] It's my secret, but you must know it.... I can't keep silence...

Pause.

I'm in love, I'm in love.... I'm in love with that man.... The one who was just here.... You know who I mean.... I'm in love with Vershinin...

OLGA [*goes to her bed, behind the screen*]. Stop it. Anyway, I'm not listening.

MASHA. What can I do! [*Holding her head.*] At first I thought he was so strange, and then I pitied him ... and then I fell in love with him ... fell in love with his voice, his words, his misfortunes, his two little girls...

OLGA [*behind the screen*]. I can't hear you. Whatever silly things you're saying, I can't hear.

MASHA. Oh, Olya, it's you who's the silly one. I love him – what can I do? That's my fate. My lot in life.... And he loves me too.... Oh, it's terrifying, isn't it? No, it's not good. [*Pulls* IRINA *by her hand, bringing her closer.*] Oh, my sweet.... How are we going to get through this life, what's going to become of us.... When you read some novel, it all seems so ordinary and obvious, but when you fall in love yourself, you can see that nobody knows anything and everyone must decide for himself.... My darlings, my sisters.... I've confessed to you, now I'll keep quiet.... I'll be like Gogol's madman now ... silence ... silence...

Enter ANDREI *followed by* FERAPONT.

ANDREI [*angrily*]. What do you want? I don't understand.

FERAPONT [*at the doors, impatiently*]. I've told you already, Mr Andrei, ten times at least.

ANDREI. First of all, you don't call me "Mr Andrei". You're supposed to say "Your Honour".

FERAPONT. Yes, Your Honour. The firemen want to know if they may cut through the garden to get to the river. Otherwise they have to go round the long way and it's a lot of trouble. Your Honour.

ANDREI. All right then. Tell them they may.

Exit FERAPONT.

Had enough of them all. Where's Olga?

OLGA *comes out from behind the screen.*

I've come to ask you for the key to the cupboard, I've lost mine. You've got the little key.

OLGA *gives him the key without saying a word.* IRINA *goes behind her screen; pause.*

Heck of a fire, eh? It's starting to die down now. God, he made me so mad, that Ferapont. That was so stupid, what I said to him.... Your Honour...

Pause.

Why don't you say something, Olya?

Pause.

It's time to stop all this moping around, all this sulking in corners. You're here Masha, Irina is here, that's perfect – let's have it out, once and for all. Clear the air! What do you have against me, eh? What is it?

OLGA. Let it go now, Andryusha. We'll talk tomorrow. [*Getting agitated.*] When will this nightmare be over!

ANDREI [*he is very embarrassed*]. Don't get upset. I'm asking you calmly, in a reasonable tone of voice: what do you have against me? Speak up.

VERSHININ'S *voice: "Tam-tam-tam!"*

MASHA [*gets up, calling out*]. Tra-ta-ta! [*To* OLGA.] Good-bye, Olya, God bless you! [*Goes behind the screen, kisses* IRINA.] Sweet dreams.... Good-bye, Andrei. Go now, they're tired.... You can settle things in the morning. [*Exits.*]

Act III

OLGA. That's right, Andryusha, let's put it off till tomorrow... [*Goes behind her screen.*] It's time for bed.

ANDREI. I'm going to speak my piece and then I'll go. Now.... First, you have a problem with Natasha, my wife. I've been aware of that since the day we were married. Natasha is a wonderful person, honest, straightforward, decent – that's my opinion. I love and respect my wife, you understand, I respect her and I demand that others respect her too. I'll say it again, she's an honest and a good person, and all your little resentments, if I may say, that's just a lot of airs and graces on your part.

Pause.

Secondly, you seem to be angry with me because I'm not a professor, not doing anything scholarly. But I work for the District Council, I'm a member of the District Council, and this duty I consider just as sacred and important as serving science. I'm a member of the District Council and I'm proud of it, if you'd like to know...

Pause.

Thirdly.... I have something else to say.... I've mortgaged the house without asking your permission.... I'm guilty of that, yes, and I'm asking for forgiveness.... My debts made me do it ... thirty-five thousand.... I don't play cards any more, I quit a long time ago, but what I can say in my defence is that you girls get a pension, and I don't receive any ... income, so to speak...

Pause.

KULYGIN [*through the door*]. Masha isn't here? [*Anxious.*] But where is she? That's strange... [*Exit.*]

ANDREI. They're not listening. Natasha is a fine upstanding person. [*Walks up and down, then stops.*] When I got married, I thought that we would all be happy ... all of us.... But my God.... [*Weeps.*] My dearest sisters, my sweet sisters, don't believe me, don't... [*Exit.*]

KULYGIN [*through the door anxiously*]. Where's Masha? Masha's not here? That's very surprising. [*Exit.*]

Sound of fire bells, the stage is empty.

IRINA [*behind the screen*]. Olya! Who is knocking on the floor?

OLGA. That's the Doctor. He's drunk.

IRINA. What a dreadful night!

Pause.

Olya! [*She looks out from behind the screen.*]

ACT III

Have you heard? They're taking the brigade away from us, they're being transferred some place far away.

OLGA. It's just rumours.

IRINA. We'll be left all alone then.... Olya!

OLGA. What?

IRINA. Dear Olya, my dear sister, I do respect the Baron, and I do value him, he's a wonderful person, and I'll marry him, I'll do it, only we must go to Moscow! I beg you, we must go! There is no place like Moscow in the whole world! We must go, Olya! We must go!

CURTAIN

ACT IV

*The Prozorovs' garden. A long avenue of fir trees,
leading to the river. On the other side of the river
is a forest. To the right is the terrace of the house.
There is a table, with glasses and a champagne
bottle. It is noon. Passers-by appear, cutting
through the garden to the river. Five* SOLDIERS
march through quickly.

CHEBUTYKIN, *in a good mood, which doesn't leave
him during the entire act, is sitting in an armchair in the garden, waiting to be called; he is
wearing a uniform cap and holding a walking
cane.* KULYGIN *(clean-shaven and wearing a medal
around his neck),* IRINA *and* TUZENBACH *are on the
terrace, saying good-bye to* FEDOTIK *and* ROHDE,
both of them in their marching uniforms.

TUZENBACH [*embracing and kissing* FEDOTIK].
    You're a good man, we've had fun. [*Embrac-
    ing and kissing* ROHDE.] One more time...
    Good-bye, dear friends!

IRINA. *Au revoir!*

FEDOTIK. It's not *au revoir*, it's "good-bye," we're
    never going to see each other again.

KULYGIN. Who knows! [*Wipes his eyes, smiles.*]
    There, now I'm crying.

ACT IV

IRINA. We'll meet again some day.

FEDOTIK. What, in ten, fifteen years? We'll barely recognize each other, we'll just nod politely and look the other way. [*Takes a picture.*] Wait.... One last time...

ROHDE [*embraces* TUZENBACH]. We're not going to see each other again... [*Kisses* IRINA*'s hand.*] Thank you. Thank you for everything!

FEDOTIK [*annoyed*]. Stand still a moment!

TUZENBACH. God willing, we'll meet again. Write to us. You must.

ROHDE [*looks the garden over*]. Good-bye, trees! [*Shouts.*] Hup-hup!

> *Pause.*

Good-bye, echo!

KULYGIN. You might get yourself a wife over there in Poland, God save you. A nice little Polish lady who will hug you and call you "Kochany!" [*Laughs.*]

FEDOTIK [*looking at his watch*]. Less than an hour left. Solyony is the only one of our battery leaving by barge, the rest of us are going on foot. Three batteries leave today, three more tomorrow – then it will be peaceful and calm in town.

TUZENBACH. And deadly dull.

ROHDE. And where is your dear wife?

KULYGIN. Masha's in the garden.

FEDOTIK. We must say good-bye to her.

ROHDE. Good-bye, I should be going, or else I'll start crying... [*Embraces* TUZENBACH *and* KULYGIN *quickly, kisses Irina's hand.*] We've had a wonderful time here...

FEDOTIK [*to* KULYGIN]. This is for you, a souvenir ... it's a little notebook with a pencil.... We'll go down to the river this way...

> *They walk away, both of them looking back.*

ROHDE [*shouts*]. Hup-hup!

KULYGIN [*shouts*]. Good-bye!

> *At the back of the stage* FEDOTIK *and* ROHDE *meet* MASHA *and say good-bye to her; she exits with them.*

IRINA. They're gone... [*Sits down on the bottom step of the verandah.*]

CHEBUTYKIN. They forgot to say good-bye to me.

IRINA. And what about you?

CHEBUTYKIN. Well, yes, I forgot too. Anyway, I'll see them soon, I'm leaving tomorrow. Yes.... One more day left. In a year they'll give me my discharge, I'll come back here and live out my life beside you.... Only one more year till I get my pension... [*Puts one newspaper into his pocket, takes out another.*] I'll come back here to you and lead a completely different life.... I'll be so nice and respectable. Pious. Quiet.

IRINA. Yes, you really should reform your ways, Doctor. It's time.

CHEBUTYKIN. I know. I know. [*Sings quietly.*] Ta-ra-ra-boom-be-ay, sit on a tomb-be-ay.

KULYGIN. You're incorrigible, Ivan Romanych! Incorrigible!

CHEBUTYKIN. Yes, if only I'd had you as a teacher. You'd have straightened me out.

IRINA. Fyodor's shaved off his moustache. I can't stand to look at him

KULYGIN. Why?

CHEBUTYKIN. I could tell you what your face looks like, but you wouldn't like it.

KULYGIN. Now, now. These things must be done. *Modus vivendi.* Our headmaster had his moustache shaved, and I did the same when I became an inspector, shaved it off. Nobody likes it, but I don't care. I'm a happy man. With or without a moustache, I'm just as happy. [*Sits down.*]

>   At the far end of the garden, ANDREI *pushes a carriage with a sleeping baby.*

IRINA. Ivan Romanych, dear heart, I'm very worried. You were on the boulevard yesterday, tell me, what happened there?

CHEBUTYKIN. What happened? Nothing. Nothing important. [*Reads a newspaper.*] It doesn't matter!

KULYGIN. The story I heard was that Solyony and the Baron met yesterday on the boulevard outside the theatre...

TUZENBACH. Stop it! It was nothing, really... [*Waves his hand and exits into the house.*]

KULYGIN. Outside the theatre.... Solyony was pestering the Baron again, the Baron had had enough, and said something insulting in return...

CHEBUTYKIN. I don't know. It's all nonsense.

KULYGIN. In some seminary, a teacher once wrote "nonsense" on an essay, but his handwriting was so bad the student thought it said "mouse fuse". [*Laughs.*] "Mouse fuse". Hilarious. The story is that Solyony is in love with Irina and that now he despises the Baron. That's easy to understand. Irina is a good girl. She's a bit like Masha, head in the clouds. Only Irina's personality is a little softer. Although, you know, Masha's got a nice personality too. I love her, my Masha.

At the back of the garden, offstage: "Yoo-hoo! Hup-hup".

IRINA [*shivering*]. Every little thing makes me jump today.

Pause.

My bags and belongings are packed and ready to go. They're going to be sent off after lunch. The Baron and I will be married tomorrow, and then we're going straight to the brickyard, and the day after that I'll be at the school, and my new life will begin. God will give me strength! When I was taking my teacher's exam, I felt tears of joy come into my eyes. I felt blessed.

Pause.

The cart will be here soon for my things.

KULYGIN. Yes, it's all very well in theory, but somehow I can't quite believe it. Highly commendable. Not very practical. But anyway, I wish you luck with all my heart.

CHEBUTYKIN [*affectionately*]. My sweet little girl, my dear child ... treasure.... You're so far ahead of me, I can't keep up. I'm left behind, like an old gander that's too feeble to fly south. Fly away, my darlings, fly away and may God give you joy!

Pause.

Big mistake shaving your moustache.

KULYGIN. All right you've made your point! [*Sighs.*]

Well, today the soldiers go, and everything will be as it was. Whatever they say, Masha is a good, honest woman, and I love her very much and I'm grateful for my good fortune. Everyone has his own path in life. There's this fellow Kozyrev who works at the tax department. We were at school together, but he never made it out of the fifth grade, because he couldn't understand the Latin rule for *ut consecutivum.* Now he's barely making a living, his health is bad, and whenever I see him, I just say: "Hey there, *ut consecutivum!*" "Yes," he says, "that's right, *ut consecutivum,*" and coughs.... Whereas I've been always been lucky, I'm happy, I've been decorated with the order of Stanislav, second class, and now I myself teach *ut consecutivum.* Of course, I'm smart, smarter than most, but that's not what happiness consists of.

In the house, someone is playing "The Maiden's Prayer".

IRINA. After tomorrow I won't be hearing the "The Maiden's Prayer" ever again, I won't be running into Protopopov...

Pause.

He's sitting in the living-room right now. Protopopov...

KULYGIN. Has our headmistress arrived yet?

ACT IV

IRINA. No. She's been sent for. It's been so hard being here alone, without Olya.... Now that she's headmistress she lives at the school; and she has her work to keep her busy, but I'm lonely, I'm bored, I've nothing to do, and I hate the room I live in.... So I've decided: if I'm not to live in Moscow, so be it. That's my fate. Nothing you can do about it.... Everything is in God's hands. The Baron asked me to marry him.... So – I thought it over and made my decision. He's a good person, he's really an astonishingly good person.... And suddenly, it's as if my soul grew wings. I cheered up, I felt as though a huge weight had been lifted from my shoulders, and once again I wanted to work, to work.... Only something happened yesterday, I can't shake this feeling of dread...

CHEBUTYKIN. It's nonsense.

NATASHA [*through the window*]. Our headmistress is here!

KULYGIN. Our headmistress is here. Let's go.

Exits with IRINA *into the house.*

CHEBUTYKIN [*reads a newspaper, sings softly*]. Ta-ra-ra ... boom-be-ay ... sit on a tomb-be-ay...

MASHA comes closer; ANDREI *pushes a stroller at the rear of the stage.*

MASHA. You just sit there, lounging around...

CHEBUTYKIN. So?

MASHA [*sits down*]. Nothing...

Pause.

Did you love my mother?

CHEBUTYKIN. Very much.

MASHA. Did she love you?

CHEBUTYKIN [*after a pause*]. That I don't remember.

MASHA. My man here? That's how, a long time ago, our cook Marfa used to talk about her policeman: "my man". My man here?

CHEBUTYKIN. Not yet.

MASHA. When you get happiness in bits and pieces, as I have, and then lose it, you become bitter and coarse. [*Points to her breast.*] I'm boiling in here... [*Looking at her brother* ANDREI, *who is pushing a carriage.*] There's Andrei, our lovely brother.... All hope is gone. Thousands of people were hoisting a bell, a lot of money and effort had been spent, and suddenly it fell down and broke apart. Suddenly, for no reason. The same with Andrei...

ANDREI. When are they going to pipe down in the house. It's so noisy.

CHEBUTYKIN. Soon. [*Looks at his watch.*] I've got an antique watch, it tells the hour... [*He winds the watch, it strikes.*] The first, the second, and the fifth batteries will leave at exactly one...

Pause.

And I'll go tomorrow.

ANDREI. For good?

CHEBUTYKIN. I don't know. Perhaps, I'll be back in a year. Although, God knows ... it makes no difference...

In the distance, a harp and a violin are playing.

ANDREI. The town will be so quiet. As if someone had put a lid on it.

Pause.

Something happened near the theatre yesterday; everyone's talking about it, and I don't know what it is.

CHEBUTYKIN. Nothing. A lot of fooferah. Solyony started to pick on the Baron, and the Baron blew up and insulted him, so Solyony ended up having to challenge the Baron to a duel. [*Looks at his watch.*] It's just about time.... At half past twelve, in the forest across the river, that one there.... Bang-bang. [*Laughs.*] Solyony thinks he's another Ler-

103

montov, he even writes poetry. A joke is a joke, but this is his third duel.

MASHA. Whose?

CHEBUTYKIN. Solyony's

MASHA. And the Baron's?

CHEBUTYKIN. What about the Baron?

Pause.

MASHA. My thoughts are going round and round, I can't think clearly.... But what I'm trying to say is that it shouldn't be allowed. He might wound the Baron or even kill him.

CHEBUTYKIN. The Baron is a good person, but one baron more, one baron less – what's the difference? Let them! What's the difference!

Someone is shouting behind the garden: "Yoo-hoo! Hup-hup".

They can wait. That's Skvortsov shouting, the second. He's waiting in the boat.

Pause.

ANDREI. In my opinion, taking part in a duel or attending one, even as a doctor, is immoral.

CHEBUTYKIN. It only seems so.... We're not really here, the world doesn't exist, we don't exist, it's all an illusion.... And anyway, what's the difference!

MASHA. Blah-blah-blah all day long... [*Walks.*] You're stuck with this climate, the snow will be on top of us any day now, and then you have to listen to this endless blathering... [*Stopping.*] I won't set foot in that house, I can't go in there.... Tell me when Vershinin comes... [*Walks up the path.*] And the birds are flying south already. [*Looks up.*] Swans or geese.... Fly away loves. Lucky ones. [*Exit.*]

ANDREI. Our house will be an empty shell. The officers will leave, you'll leave, my sister will get married, and it'll be just me in the house.

CHEBUTYKIN. What about your wife?

Enter FERAPONT *with papers.*

ANDREI. A wife is a wife. She's honest, decent ... kind – I guess – but at the same time there's something so degraded about her that reminds me of a ... grubby, blind, some sort of scaly animal. Whatever it is, she's not human. I'm telling this to you as a friend, the only person I can open my heart to. I love Natasha, I do, but at times she seems to me unbelievably squalid, and then I'm lost, I don't understand why, or how I could love her or at least used to love...

CHEBUTYKIN [*gets up*]. My friend, I'm leaving tomorrow, we might never see each other again, so listen carefully to what I say. Put your hat on your head, take your stick in hand, and walk out the door. Don't look back. Just keep walking. The farther you go, the better.

> SOLYONY *crosses the far end of the stage with two* OFFICERS; *as he sees* CHEBUTYKIN, *he turns to him; the officers continue to walk.*

SOLYONY. Doctor, it's time! It's already half past twelve. [*Says hello to* ANDREI.]

CHEBUTYKIN. In a minute, for God's sake. I'm sick to death of all this. [*To* ANDREI.] Andryusha. If anyone wants me, say that I'll be right back... [*Sighs.*] Oh-oh-oh!

SOLYONY. "Before the man had time to breathe, the bear had caught him in a squeeze." [*Walks with him.*] What are you bellyaching about, old man?

CHEBUTYKIN. For God's sake!

SOLYONY. How are you feeling?

CHEBUTYKIN [*angrily*]. Like a potato peeling!

SOLYONY. Take it easy, old man. I know what I'm doing. I'll just clip his wings, like a woodcock. [*Takes out a bottle of perfume and sprays some on his hands.*] There, I've used up the whole bottle today, but still they smell. They smell like a corpse.

Pause.

So.... Remember the verse? "Alas! It longs for storms and riot, as if a storm could bring it peace."

CHEBUTYKIN. Yes. "Before the man had time to breathe, the bear had caught him in a squeeze." [*Exit with* SOLYONY.]

> *Someone is shouting "Hup-hup! Yoo-hoo".
> Enter* ANDREI *and* FERAPONT.

FERAPONT. Papers to sign...

ANDREI [*agitated*]. Leave me alone! Let me be, for God's sake! [*He exits with a carriage.*]

FERAPONT. Isn't that what papers are for, signing? [*Retreats to the far end of the stage.*]

> *Enter* IRINA *and* TUZENBACH *in a straw hat;*
> KULYGIN *crosses the stage, shouting: "Yoo-hoo, Masha, yoo-hoo!".*

TUZENBACH. He must be the only person in town who's happy to see the soldiers go.

IRINA. That's understandable.

Pause.

Our town will soon be deserted.

TUZENBACH [*taking a look at his watch*]. My dear, I'll be back in a minute.

IRINA. Where are you going?

TUZENBACH. I just need to go into town, to ... to say good-bye to some people.

IRINA. That's not true.... Nikolai, why are you so distracted today?

Pause.

What happened yesterday near the theatre?

TUZENBACH [*an impatient gesture*]. In an hour I'll be back with you again. [*Kisses her hands.*] My beloved... [*Looks into her face.*] I've loved you for five years now, and I still can't get used to it. Each time I see you, you're more beautiful than before. Your beautiful hair. Amazing eyes. Tomorrow we'll drive away together, we'll go to work, we'll be rich, all my dreams will have come true. And you will be happy. Except for one thing: you don't love me.

IRINA. It's not in my power. I'll be your wife, faithful and true, but there's no love, and there's nothing I can do about it! [*Weeps.*] I have never loved anyone in my life. I've dreamed about love, I've dreamed about it for years, day and night, but my soul is like an expensive grand piano, locked up and the key is lost.

Pause.

You look so unhappy.

TUZENBACH. I didn't sleep well last night. There's nothing terrible in my life, I'm not afraid of anything, it's just this lost key that tears at my heart, won't let me sleep.... Say something to me.

Pause.

Say something to me...

IRINA. What? What should I say? What?

TUZENBACH. Something.

IRINA. All right. All right.

Pause.

TUZENBACH. What silly things, what trivial things, can suddenly, for no reason, make such a difference in your life. You shrug them off, make fun of them, and yet you feel you're in the grip of something too powerful to resist. Oh, let's not talk about it! I feel very cheerful. I'm looking at those fir trees, those maple trees and birch trees, and it's as if I'm seeing them for the first time. And everything seems to be looking back at me, curiously. Waiting. What beautiful trees, and really, how beautiful life ought to be beside them.

Someone shouts, "Yoo-hoo! Hup-hup!"

I must go, it's time.... See, there's a birch tree that has died, but still it sways in the wind along with the others. So it seems to me, if I should die, I'd still be a part of life one way or another. Good-bye, my darling... [*Kisses her hands.*] The papers you gave me are on my desk under the calendar.

IRINA. I'm coming with you.

TUZENBACH [*alarmed*]. No, no! [*Walks away quickly, then stops in the middle of the path.*] Irina!

IRINA. What?

TUZENBACH [*not knowing what to say*]. Irina. I haven't had coffee today. Would you tell them to make me some... [*Quickly exits.*]

> IRINA *stands deep in thought, then goes to the far end of the stage and sits down on the swing. Enter* ANDREI *with a carriage;* FERAPONT *appears.*

FERAPONT. It's not for me, you know, they're not my papers, they're from the District Council.

ANDREI. Oh, where has it gone, where has it gone, my glorious past, when I was young and clever and carefree, full of grand ideas, when the world seemed overflowing with possibilities? How is it that, almost before we've begun to live, the door slams on all that and we become dull, stupid, lazy, boring and miserable.... Our town has been around for two hundred years now, there are a hundred thousand people living here, and not a single one that isn't like the others, not a single saint, past or present, not a single scholar, not a single artist, not a single remotely distinguished person who could stir the least envy or desire to emulate him.... All they do is eat, drink, sleep, and then die ... others are born and they too eat, drink and sleep, and to keep from becoming paralyzed with boredom, they spice up their lives with gossip and vodka, card-games and lawsuits; the wives cheat their husbands, and the husbands turn a blind eye, pretend they see nothing, hear nothing, and this murk of lies infects the children, and the divine spark is extinguished in them, and they become the same pitiful walking corpses as their fathers and mothers... [*To* FERAPONT *angrily*]. What the hell do you want?

FERAPONT. What's that? Papers to sign.

ANDREI. I'm sick and tired of you.

FERAPONT [*giving him papers*]. The doorman at the courthouse was telling me just now.... What was it? Last winter, he says, in St Petersburg, it was two hundred degrees below zero.

ANDREI. The present is unbearable, but when I think of the future, I feel better! I can breathe again, my body feels easier, there's a light on the horizon; I see freedom, I see myself and my children freed from idleness, from vodka, from goose with cabbage, from naps after lunch, from sponging off others...

FERAPONT. Two thousand people froze up solid, he says. Two thousand frozen stiffs, he says. Was it Petersburg or Moscow? – Can't remember now.

ANDREI [*overcome by a feeling of tenderness*]. My dear sisters, my lovely sisters! [*Through the tears.*] Masha, my sweet sister...

NATASHA [*in the window*]. Who's that talking so loudly out there? Is it you, Andryusha? You'll wake up Sophochka.... *Il ne faut pas faire du bruit, la Sophie est dormée déjà. Vous êtes un ours.* [*Furious.*] If you want to talk, give the baby carriage to someone else. Ferapont, take the baby carriage from the master!

FERAPONT. Yes missus. [*Takes the carriage.*]

ANDREI [*embarrassed*]. I was speaking softly.

NATASHA [*behind the window, playing with her child*]. Bobik! Who's a bad boy? Bad Bobik!

ANDREI [*looking over the papers*]. Fine, I'll look them over and sign what has to be signed, and you can take them back to the Council... [*Exit into the house reading the papers; FERAPONT pushes the carriage towards the*

Act IV

back of the garden.]

NATASHA [*behind the window*]. Bobik, what's mummy's name? Good *boy*! And who's that? That's your aunt Olya, say "Hello Auntie Olya!"

> *Two street* MUSICIANS, *a man and a young girl, play the violin and the harp;* VERSHININ, OLGA *and* ANFISA *come out of the house and listen for a minute in silence;* IRINA *draws near to them.*

OLGA. Our garden has become a public thoroughfare; everyone comes through here. Nanny, give the musicians something!...

ANFISA [*gives some money to the* MUSICIANS]. Off you go, now, God bless.

> MUSICIANS *bow and exit.*

Poor things. They wouldn't hang around here if they had food in their bellies. [*To* IRINA.] Good day, Irinushka [*Kisses her.*] Ahhh, child, the life I lead! The life I lead! In the school building, a government apartment, living with Olyushka – that's how God's decided I should end my days. Never in my life did I expect to live like this, sinner that I am.... Big apartment, government subsidized, and I've got my own room and a little bed. I don't pay for a thing. I wake up at night and – oh, gracious God, Mother of God, no one is happier than I!

113

VERSHININ [*taking a look at his watch*]. We have to leave, now. It's time.

Pause.

I wish you the best of everything.... Where is Masha?

IRINA. Somewhere in the garden.... I'll go look for her.

VERSHININ. If you please. I'm in a hurry.

ANFISA. I'll help you look. [*Shouts.*] Mashenka, yoo-hoo! [*Exit together with Irina into far end of the garden.*] Yoo-hoo, yoo-hoo!

VERSHININ. Everything comes to an end. And now it's our turn to part. [*Looks at his watch.*] The town gave us a luncheon, we drank champagne, the mayor made a speech. All the time I was eating and listening, but my soul was here, with you... [*Looks around the garden.*] I've grown accustomed to all of you.

OLGA. Will we ever see each other again?

VERSHININ. Probably not.

Pause.

My wife and little girls are staying on for another two months; please, if something should happen or if they need anything...

OLGA. Yes, yes, of course. Don't worry.

Pause.

Tomorrow there won't be a single officer in town, it will all be just a memory. And for us, of course, a new life will begin...

Pause.

Nothing turns out the way we intend it. I didn't want to be headmistress, but that's what I've become. And, it seems, we won't ever get to Moscow...

VERSHININ. Well.... Thank you for everything.... Forgive me if I did anything wrong.... I know that I talked much too much – forgive me for that too, don't think badly of me.

OLGA [*wiping her eyes*]. Why isn't Masha here...

VERSHININ. What else can I say to you by way of farewell? What's left to philosophize about?... [*Laughs.*] Life is hard. For many of us it seems hopelessly bleak, but we have to admit that life on earth is getting clearer and brighter all the time, and surely the time is coming when everything will at last be bright as day. [*Looks at his watch.*] It's time for me, it's time! Mankind used to be busy with wars, filling its existence with marches, invasions, victories; now all that is past, leaving behind an enormous void, which we haven't yet found a way to fill; but mankind is searching desperately and one day, of course, we will find it. Oh, if only it would be soon!

Pause.

You know, if it were possible to add education to diligence, and diligence to education. [*Looks at his watch.*] Anyway, I must be going...

OLGA. There she is.

Enter MASHA.

VERSHININ. I came to say good-bye...

> OLGA *steps aside a little not to spoil their good-bye.*

MASHA [*looking into his face*]. Good-bye. My beloved.

A long kiss.

OLGA. There, there...

> MASHA *is sobbing violently.*

VERSHININ. Write to me.... Don't forget! Let me go ... it's time.... Olga, please take her, I must ... it's time.... I'm late... [*Moved, kisses* OLGA*'s hands, than hugs* MASHA *one more time and quickly goes.*]

OLGA. There, there Masha! Stop crying now, darling...

Enter KULYGIN.

ACT IV

KULYGIN [*embarrassed*]. That's all right, let her
cry, that's all right.... My good, kind
Masha.... You are my wife, and I'm happy,
whatever may be.... I'm not complaining, I'm
not reproaching you for a single thing....
Here, let Olya be my witness.... We'll go
back to our old life, and I won't say a single
word, not a whisper...

MASHA [*holding back her sobs*]. "Beside the sea a
green oak's standing / and on it hangs a
golden chain" ... "and on it hangs a golden
chain" ... I'm going out of my mind.... Beside the sea ... a green oak's standing.

OLGA. Calm down, Masha.... Calm down.... Give
her some water.

MASHA. I'm not crying any more...

KULYGIN. She isn't crying any more.... She's a good
girl.

Sound of a muffled, far-away shot.

MASHA. Beside the sea a green oak's standing /
and on it hangs a golden chain ... cat's green
... oak's green ... I mix them up... [*Drinks
the water.*] A wasted life.... I don't need anything now.... I'll calm down in a second....
It doesn't matter.... What does it mean "beside the sea, the curving strand"? Why is
this word in my head? My thoughts are getting all mixed up.

Enter IRINA.

OLGA. Calm down, Masha. There, that's a good girl.... Let's go in.

MASHA [*angrily*]. I'm not setting foot in there. [*Sobs, but stops immediately.*] I don't go into that house any more...

IRINA. Let's sit together for a moment, and just be quiet. I'm leaving tomorrow...

Pause.

KULYGIN. Look what I took from a boy in third grade... [*Puts on the moustache and beard.*] I look like the German teacher... [*Laughs.*] Don't you think? Real cut-ups, those boys.

MASHA. Yes, you do look like the German teacher.

OLGA [*laughs*]. Yes.

MASHA *cries.*

IRINA. Enough, Masha!

KULYGIN. Look just like him...

Enter NATASHA.

NATASHA [*to the* MAID]. What? Protopopov will mind Sophochka, and Andrei can push Bobik in the carriage. Children! They're a constant headache... [*To* IRINA.] Irina, you're leaving tomorrow – such a pity. Won't you stay one more week? [*Noticing* KULYGIN, *she*

*screams; he laughs and takes off his mous-
tache and beard.*] You scared me to death.
[*To* IRINA.] I'm so used to you, it's not going
to be easy here without you. I'll have Andrei
move into your room with his violin – he
can saw away in there! – Sophochka can go
in his room. Such a cutie! And so smart!
Today she looked at me with those big eyes
and said – "mama"!

KULYGIN. She's a remarkable child, it's true.

NATASHA. So tomorrow I'll be all alone here.
[*Sighs.*] First of all I'm going to have them
chop down those fir trees along the path,
and then that maple.... It's a terrible eye-
sore in the evening... [*To* IRINA.] Darling,
that belt doesn't suit you at all.... It's
dreary.... You need something brighter. And
right here I'm going to have them plant
those little flowers that smell so nice...
[*Sternly.*] What's this fork doing out here
on the bench? [*Going into the house, to the*
MAID.] I said, what is this fork doing on the
bench? [*Shouts.*] Don't you talk back to me!

KULYGIN. There she goes again!

*There is music offstage playing a march;
everyone is listening.*

OLGA. They're leaving.

Enter CHEBUTYKIN.

MASHA. Our men are leaving. Well ... Happy journey to them! [*To her husband.*] We should go home.... Where are my hat and cloak?

KULYGIN. I took them inside.... I'll get them. [*Exit into the house.*]

OLGA. Yes, we can go home now. It's time.

CHEBUTYKIN. Olga!

OLGA. What?

> *Pause.*

What?

CHEBUTYKIN. Nothing.... I don't know how to tell you... [*Whispers in her ear.*]

OLGA [*frightened*]. I don't believe it!

CHEBUTYKIN. Yes.... A nasty business.... Ach! I'm worn out, I'm exhausted, I don't want to talk about it [*Annoyed.*] Anyway, what's the difference!

MASHA. What happened?

OLGA [*hugging* IRINA]. What a dreadful day.... I don't know how to tell you this, my darling...

IRINA. What? Tell me now, what? For God's sake! [*Cries.*]

CHEBUTYKIN. The Baron has just been killed in a duel...

ACT IV

IRINA [*cries softly*]. I knew it, I knew it...

CHEBUTYKIN [*sits on the bench at the back of the stage*]. Worn out... [*Takes a newspaper out of his pocket.*] Let them have their little cry... [*Sings softly.*] Ta-ra-ra-boom-be-ay ... sit on a tomb-be-ay. Anyway, it doesn't matter!

The three sisters stand huddled together.

MASHA. Oh, listen to the band! They're going, they're leaving now, one is gone forever, and we will stay here to start our life over. We must live.... We must live...

IRINA [*puts her head on* OLGA*'s breast*]. The time will come when everyone will know what all this is for, this suffering; and then there will be no more secrets, but until then we must live, we must work, just work! Tomorrow I'll go by myself to the brickworks, I'll teach at the school and I'll give my whole life to those who might need it. It's autumn now, soon it will be winter, everything will be covered with snow, and I will be working, working...

OLGA [*hugs both her sisters*]. The band is playing so cheerfully, so joyfully, you want to live! O God! God! Time will pass, and we will disappear forever, we will be forgotten, our faces, our voices, how many we were; but our suffering will turn to joy for those who live after us; peace and happiness will descend on the Earth, and they will speak kindly of us and bless those who live now. Oh, my dear sisters, our life is not over yet. We will live! The music sounds so cheerful, so joyful, and it seems that any minute now we will know what we are living for, and why we suffer.... If only we knew, if only we knew!

The music is playing softer and softer; Kulygin, *happy and smiling, brings the hat and the cloak;* Andrei *pushes the carriage with* Bobik *in it.*

Chebutykin [*sings softly*]. Tara ... ra ... boom-be-ay ... sit on a tomb-be-ay... [*Reads a newspaper.*] What does it matter? What does it matter?

Olga. If only we knew, if only we knew!

CURTAIN